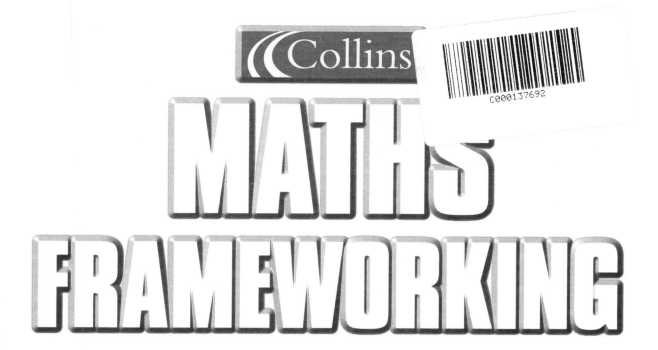

Collins

MATHS FRAMEWORKING

Complete success for Mathematics at KS3

YEAR 9   PRACTICE BOOK 1

ANDREW EDMONDSON

Contents

1A Simple sequences

1 Work through the flow diagrams. For each one:
  i Write down the results as a sequence.
  ii Describe the sequence, including the term-to-term rule.

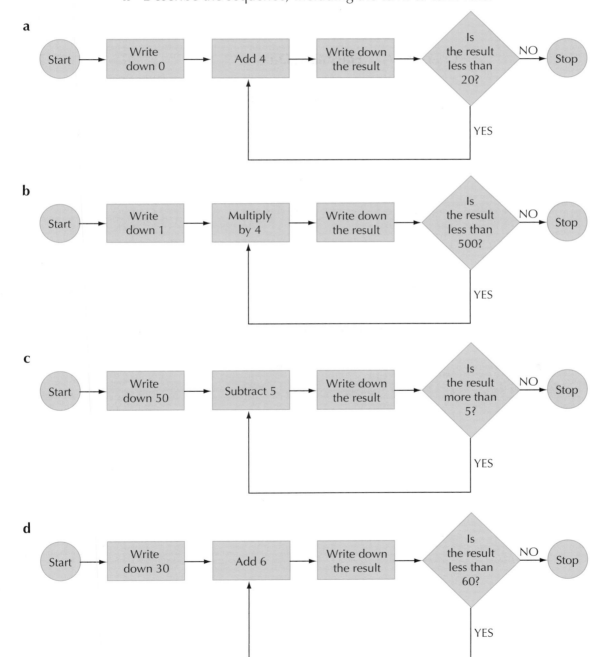

a

Start → Write down 0 → Add 4 → Write down the result → Is the result less than 20? — NO → Stop / YES

b

Start → Write down 1 → Multiply by 4 → Write down the result → Is the result less than 500? — NO → Stop / YES

c

Start → Write down 50 → Subtract 5 → Write down the result → Is the result more than 5? — NO → Stop / YES

d

Start → Write down 30 → Add 6 → Write down the result → Is the result less than 60? — NO → Stop / YES

2 For each of the following sequences:
    i Write down the term-to-term rule.
    ii Draw a flow diagram that gives the sequence.

  a 10, 20, 30, 40, 50
  b 50, 48, 46, 44, 42, 40

3 Work through the flow diagrams.
Write down the results as a sequence.

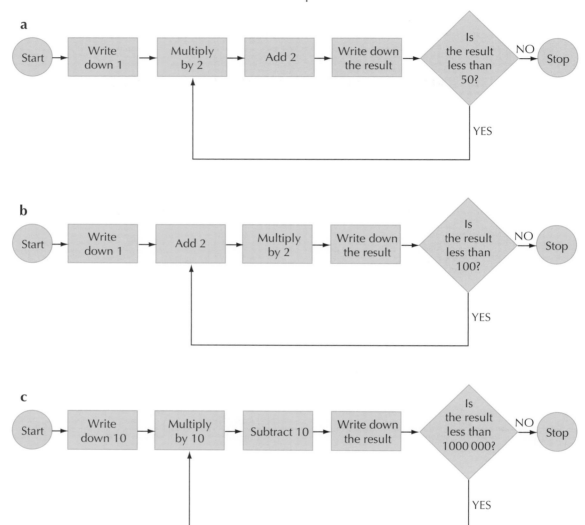

For questions 1 to 3:
a Draw the next two shapes.
b Write down the numbers of dots in each pattern.
c Write down the term-to-term rule.

1

d Find the number of dots in the 10th pattern without drawing it.

2

d Find the number of dots in the 30th pattern without drawing it.

3

d Find the number of dots in the 20th pattern without drawing it.

4 Dots 3
Lines 3

a Draw the next two shapes.
b Write down the numbers of lines and dots in each pattern.
c Write down the term-to-term rule for the number of:
　i dots　　　　　ii lines
d Without drawing the shapes
　i find the number of dots in the 25th pattern
　ii find the number of lines in the 15th pattern.

1 The nth term of a sequence is $3n + 4$.

    a Find the first 5 terms of the sequence.
    b Find: **i** the 10th term   **ii** the 40th term.

2 The nth term of a sequence is $120 - 2n$.

    a Find the first 5 terms of the sequence.
    b Find the **i** 20th   **ii** 45th terms.

3 The nth term of a sequence is $10n - 5$.

    a Find the first 5 terms of the sequence.
    b Find the **i** 18th   **ii** 100th terms.

4 Find the nth term for each sequence.

a

Position number, n	1	2	3	4	5
Term	5	10	15	20	25

b

Position number, n	1	2	3	4	5
Term	8	9	10	11	12

c

Position number, n	1	2	3	4	5
Term	0	1	2	3	4

5 For each sequence:

    i copy and complete the table below.

Position number, n	1	2	3	4	5
Term					

    ii Find the nth term.

    a 4, 8, 12, 16, 20 ...   **b** 11, 12, 13, 14, 15 ...

6 Look at these shapes.

Shape 1   Shape 2   Shape 3

    a Copy and complete the table.

Shape, n	1	2	3	4
Number of orange lines				
Number of black lines				
Total number of lines				

b i Write down the nth term for the number of orange lines.
  ii How many orange lines are there in the 25th shape?
c i Write down the nth term for the number of black lines.
  ii How many black lines are there in the 75th shape?
d The nth term for the total number of lines is $3n + 1$.
  How many lines are there in the 50th shape?

Practice

1D Combination functions and mappings

1 For each input, copy and complete the mapping diagrams by filling in the boxes.

a input → multiply by 4 → add 6 x → $4x + 6$

0 → ☐ → ☐ 0 → ☐

1 → 4 → 10 1 → 10

2 → ☐ → ☐ 2 → ☐

3 → ☐ → ☐ 3 → ☐

b input → multiply by 3 → subtract 2 x → $3x - 2$

1 → ☐ → ☐ 1 → ☐

2 → ☐ → ☐ 2 → ☐

3 → ☐ → ☐ 3 → ☐

4 → ☐ → ☐ 4 → ☐

c input → add 10 → multiply by 3 x → $3(x + 10)$

0 → ☐ → ☐ 0 → ☐

1 → ☐ → ☐ 1 → ☐

2 → ☐ → ☐ 2 → ☐

3 → ☐ → ☐ 3 → ☐

2 a x → $5x - 1$

1 → ☐

2 → ☐

3 → ☐

4 → ☐

b x → $3(x + 4)$

0 → ☐

1 → ☐

2 → ☐

3 → ☐

3 Draw a mapping diagram using these inputs: $x = 1$, $x = 2$, $x = 3$, $x = 4$.

  a $x \rightarrow 3x + 7$ b $x \rightarrow 2(x + 4)$

4 Copy and complete the combined mapping diagram on the right for each function.

$x \rightarrow$ [   ]

$1 \rightarrow$ [   ]

$2 \rightarrow$ [   ]

$3 \rightarrow$ [   ]

$4 \rightarrow$ [   ]

  a input $\rightarrow$ multiply by 6 $\rightarrow$ subtract 2 $\rightarrow$ output

  b input $\rightarrow$ add 8 $\rightarrow$ multiply by 4 $\rightarrow$ output

5 Copy and complete these mapping diagrams.

  a input $\rightarrow$ [   ] $\rightarrow$ [   ] $\rightarrow$ output

  1 $\rightarrow$ 2 $\rightarrow$ [   ] $\rightarrow$ 1

  2 $\rightarrow$ 4 $\rightarrow$ [   ] $\rightarrow$ 3

  3 $\rightarrow$ 6 $\rightarrow$ [   ] $\rightarrow$ 5

  4 $\rightarrow$ 8 $\rightarrow$ [   ] $\rightarrow$ 7

  b input $\rightarrow$ [   ] $\rightarrow$ [   ] $\rightarrow$ output

  0 $\rightarrow$ 5 $\rightarrow$ [   ] $\rightarrow$ 20

  1 $\rightarrow$ 6 $\rightarrow$ [   ] $\rightarrow$ 24

  2 $\rightarrow$ 7 $\rightarrow$ [   ] $\rightarrow$ 28

  3 $\rightarrow$ 8 $\rightarrow$ [   ] $\rightarrow$ 32

1 a Copy and complete the table below for the function $y = 3x$.

x		−3	−2	−1	0	1	2	3
$y = 3x$								

  b Draw a grid with its x-axis from −3 to 3 and y-axis from −10 to 10.
  c Draw the graph of the function $y = 3x$.

2 a Copy and complete the table below for the function $y = 4x - 3$.

x		0	1	2	3	4	5
$y = 4x - 3$							

  b Draw a grid with its x-axis from 0 to 5 and y-axis from −5 to 20.
  c Draw the graph of the function $y = 4x - 3$.

3 a Copy and complete the table for each of the functions.

x		−2	−1	0	1	2	3
$y = x + 2$							
$y = 2x + 2$							
$y = 3x + 2$							
$y = 4x + 2$							

  b Draw a grid with its x-axis from −2 to 3 and y-axis from −10 to 15.
  c On the axes draw the graph of each function in the table.
  d What is the same about the lines?
  e What is different about the lines?
  f Use a dotted line to sketch the graph of $y = 5x + 2$.
      Use your answers to parts **d** and **e** to help you.

CHAPTER **2** # Number 1

2A Ordering decimals

1 Convert these improper (top-heavy) fractions to mixed numbers.

a $\frac{9}{4}$ **b** $\frac{17}{2}$ **c** $\frac{13}{3}$ **d** $\frac{27}{5}$ **e** $\frac{50}{7}$

2 Write these sets of numbers in order, with the smallest first.

a 2.382, 1.893, 2.03, 2.4, 1.86
b 0.132, 0.031, 0.302, 0.123, 0.052

3 Put the correct sign > or < between these pairs of numbers.

a 3.62 … 3.26 **b** 0.07 … 0.073 **c** £0.09 … 10p

4 Put these amounts of money in order, with the smallest first: £1.20, 32p, £0.28, 23p, £0.63.

5 Put these lengths in order, with the smallest first: 57 cm, 2.05 m, 0.06 m, 123 cm, 0.9 m.

6 Write the weights of these cheeses in order, with the smallest first.
Hint: convert kilograms to grams.

785 g   0.67 kg   3.2 kg   0.652 kg   0.8 kg

2B Adding and subtracting fractions

If necessary, convert your answers to mixed numbers and cancel down.

1 Use an eighths fraction chart to calculate the following.

a $\frac{7}{8} + \frac{3}{4}$ **b** $1\frac{5}{8} + 2\frac{7}{8}$ **c** $1\frac{1}{4} - \frac{3}{8}$

d $3\frac{1}{2} - 1\frac{5}{8}$ **e** $2\frac{1}{4} + 1\frac{3}{8} - 2\frac{5}{8}$

2 Calculate the following.

a $\frac{2}{7} + \frac{3}{7}$ **b** $\frac{11}{12} - \frac{7}{12}$

c $\frac{4}{5} + \frac{3}{5} + \frac{4}{5}$ **d** $\frac{5}{8} + \frac{7}{8} - \frac{3}{8}$

3 Convert the fractions to equivalent fractions with a common denominator. Then calculate the answer.

a $\frac{1}{5} + \frac{1}{2}$ b $\frac{1}{10} + \frac{2}{5}$ c $\frac{5}{6} + \frac{4}{9}$ d $\frac{3}{8} + \frac{5}{6} + \frac{1}{4}$

e $\frac{3}{4} - \frac{1}{3}$ f $\frac{11}{12} - \frac{3}{4}$ g $\frac{7}{9} - \frac{1}{3}$ h $\frac{9}{10} - \frac{1}{2} - \frac{1}{5}$

4 $\frac{3}{5}$ of Jan's emails are junk mail and $\frac{1}{10}$ is from friends. The rest is work related.

a What fraction is work related?
b Jan received 120 emails during the week. How many were not junk mail?

5 A poster is printed using red, blue and yellow inks. Of the ink used, $\frac{2}{9}$ is red and $\frac{1}{6}$ is blue.

a What fraction of the ink used is not yellow?
b 36 ml of ink is used to print the poster. Calculate the amount of each ink used.

Practice

2C Multiplying and dividing fractions

1 Cancel these fractions. Write as a mixed fraction if necessary.

a $\frac{12}{18}$ b $\frac{20}{14}$ c $\frac{45}{75}$ d $\frac{49}{21}$ e $\frac{16}{80}$

Cancel before multiplying, if possible. Cancel your answer and write as a mixed fraction, if necessary.

2 a $\frac{4}{9} \times \frac{2}{5}$ b $\frac{5}{8} \times \frac{2}{3}$ c $\frac{8}{15} \times \frac{5}{7}$ d $\frac{10}{21} \times \frac{7}{15}$

e $\frac{9}{16} \times \frac{12}{27}$ f $\frac{15}{6} \times \frac{12}{5}$ g $\frac{20}{9} \times \frac{15}{16}$

3 a $\frac{5}{8} \div \frac{2}{3}$ b $\frac{3}{5} \div \frac{7}{10}$ c $\frac{15}{16} \div \frac{9}{10}$ d $\frac{8}{9} \div \frac{10}{21}$

e $\frac{16}{25} \div \frac{14}{15}$ f $\frac{10}{3} \div \frac{1}{6}$ g $\frac{32}{21} \div \frac{4}{9}$

4 $\frac{7}{10}$ of the surface of Earth is covered in water. $\frac{3}{14}$ of this area is the Atlantic Ocean. What fraction of the surface of the Earth is the Atlantic Ocean?

5 A bottle contains $\frac{8}{9}$ ounces of perfume. A perfume spray contains $\frac{1}{6}$ ounce of perfume. How many sprays can be filled from the bottle?

Practice

2D Integers and fractions

Calculate the following. Write the integer as a fraction with denominator 1. Cancel your answers and write as mixed numbers where necessary.

1 a $\frac{1}{9} \times 7$ b $5 \times \frac{2}{3}$ c $\frac{7}{4} \times 2$ d $10 \times \frac{3}{8}$ e $\frac{10}{9} \times 15$

2 a $\frac{1}{2} \div 4$ b $\frac{8}{9} \div 12$ c $\frac{8}{7} \div 6$ d $\frac{9}{25} \div 12$ e $\frac{100}{3} \div 20$

Work out the following questions in your head. Write down your answers.

3 **a** How many thirds are there in 4?
   b How many sixths are there in 10?

4 **a** $4 \div \frac{1}{2}$ **b** $3 \div \frac{1}{8}$ **c** $8 \div \frac{1}{10}$ **d** $5 \div \frac{1}{7}$ **e** $9 \div \frac{1}{9}$

Calculate answers to the following questions. Show your working.

5 Sue uses $\frac{2}{9}$ of a tin of polish every time she waxes her car.

   a How many car waxes will she get from 3 tins?
   b How many tins of wax will she use to wax her car 24 times?

6 A volcanic lava flow moves $\frac{2}{3}$ of a metre every hour. How long will it take to move 12 metres?

Practice **2E Ratio**

1 Cancel the following ratios to their simplest form.

   a $9 : 15$ **b** $28 : 12$ **c** $200 : 125$ **d** $44 : 121$ **e** $16 : 8 : 4$

2 Write the following ratios in the form $1 : n$.

   a $3 : 18$ **b** $10 : 25$ **c** $7 : 49$ **d** $40 : 50$ **e** $2 : 7$

3 Write the following ratios in the form $n : 1$.

   a $28 : 4$ **b** $42 : 8$ **c** $200 : 125$ **d** $4 : 5$ **e** $60 : 24$

4 The ratio of men to women attending a concert was $7 : 5$. If 228 people attended, how many of these were **(a)** men **(b)** women?

5 Catriona spends her pocket money in the following ratio:

   savings : magazines : entertainment $= 5 : 3 : 2$

   How does she spend £13.50 of pocket money?

6 A compost mixture is made from peat and garden waste in the ratio $4 : 11$.

   a How much peat does a 120 litre bag of compost mixture contain?
   b If a pile of compost mixture contains 48 litres of peat, how much garden waste does it contain?
   c How much compost mixture could be made from 60 litres of peat and 99 litres of garden waste?

7 Charities use part of their donations for running costs and the remainder for good causes. The table shows the ratios for three charities.

Charity	Running costs : Good causes
World Need	2 : 5
Pet Protection	12 : 33
Cancer Cure	8 : 21

a Change the ratios to the form 1 : n.
b Which charity gives the greatest proportion of donations to good causes?

Practice

2F Direct proportion

1 Martha takes 30 minutes to read 20 pages.
How long will it take her to read 30 pages?

2 6 boxes contain 54 light bulbs.
How many light bulbs are contained in 9 boxes?

3 The diagram shows part of a square tiled floor.

a If the floor has 54 black tiles, how many white tiles does it have?
b If the floor has 400 tiles altogether, how many white tiles does it have?

4 5 identical candles lit at the same time take 60 minutes to burn down.
How long will 9 candles take?

5 **a** 18 eggs cost a shopkeeper £2.88. How much do 10 cost?
b 60 egg boxes cost £3.90. How much do 150 cost?
c An egg box can contain 6 eggs. What is the cost of 10 boxes of eggs?

6 A value pack of sweets contains 6 Tweeny Bars, 8 Swirlies and 12 Fruitgums.
Alma bought some value packs for a party. There were 32 Swirlies altogether.

a How many Fruitgums were there?
b How many Tweeny bars were there?
Jan bought value packs containing 182 sweets altogether.
c How many Swirlies were there?

7 Jason used 6 litres of paint to cover 15 m of fence.
How much paint is needed to cover 40 m of fence?

8 6 parachutists jump out of an aeroplane and take 12 minutes to land.
How long will 8 parachutists take to land?

9 A tortoise and a hare had a race. They travelled at a constant speed. When
the tortoise had travelled 24 metres, the hare had travelled 108 metres.

    a How far had the tortoise travelled when the hare had travelled
126 metres?

    b How far had the hare travelled when the tortoise had travelled
100 metres?

    c If the hare took 4 minutes to travel 108 metres, how long did the
tortoise take?

Practice

2G Inverse proportion

1 Lai Ping has 10 rows of 18 football stickers on his bedroom wall.
He rearranges them into 12 rows. How many stickers are in each row?

2 9 people take 24 hours to sew a patchwork quilt.

    a How long would 6 people take?

    b How many people would be needed to finish the quilt in 4 hours?

3 A packet of grass seed can cover a rectangular lawn measuring 6 metres by
9 metres. Maria uses a whole packet on her lawn that is 4 metres wide.
How long is her lawn?

4 A new battery can run 3 model trains for 8 hours.
How long can it run 6 trains for?

5 During a maths lesson for 15 students, the fire alarm sounded for
20 seconds. How long will the fire alarm sound when there are 20 students
in the class?

6 An aeroplane journey took 2 hours at an average speed of 300 mph.

    a How long would it take to travel the same journey at:

        i 200 mph   **ii** 400 mph   **iii** 900 mph?

        Give your answers in hours and minutes.

    b How fast would the aeroplane need to travel to complete the journey in

        i 1 hour   **ii** 5 hours   **ii** 45 minutes?

        Hint: Convert minutes to hours first.

7 It takes 6 bricklayers 3 hours to build a wall 100 cm high.

    a How long would 4 bricklayers take to build the same wall?
    b How long would it take 6 bricklayers to build a wall 200 cm high?
    c How many bricklayers would it take to build a 180 cm wall in 2 hours?

2H Rounding and calculator displays

1 Round each number to 1 decimal place.

    a 5.26   **b** 9.848   **c** 0.275   **d** 24.08
    e 4.041   **f** 4.97   **g** 9.98

2 Round each number to 2 decimal places.

    a 2.863   **b** 10.489   **c** 9.302   **d** 0.307
    e 25.596   **f** 0.007   **g** 5.004

3 The answer on Siobhan's calculator is $\boxed{9.4^{04}}$
    Which of these numbers is the answer?

    a 940   **b** 0.00094   **c** 9400   **d** 940 000   **e** 94 000

4 The answer on Frank's calculator is $\boxed{3.1^{-02}}$
    Which of these numbers is the answer?

    a 0.031   **b** 310   **c** 0.31   **d** 0.0031   **e** 31

5 Write down the number shown on each calculator display.

    a 3.603   **b** 9.9^{04} **c** 4.13^{02} **d** 2.705   **e** $7.^{03}$

6 Write down the number shown on each calculator display.

    a 2.2^{-04} **b** 5.3^{-02} **c** $8.^{-04}$ **d** 1.96^{-03} **e** 8.2^{-05}

7 Write down the number shown on each calculator display.

    a 6.7^{03} **b** 1.1^{-02} **c** $4.^{05}$ **d** 9.52^{04} **e** 1.06^{-03}

8 Write these numbers as calculator displays.

    a 42 000   **b** 6700   **c** 920 000   **d** 3 000 000   **e** 42 500

9 Write these numbers as calculator displays.

    a 0.0034   **b** 0.092   **c** 0.000 055
    d 0.000 006   **e** 0.006 24

10 Write these numbers as calculator displays.

    a 7000   **b** 0.000 42   **c** 72 700   **d** 0.0367   **e** 0.0029

CHAPTER

3 Algebra 3

3A Formulae

Substitute numbers into each formula to answer the questions.
Show your working.

1 a Given that $M = 4n + 5$, find M when $n = 7$.
   b Given that $f = a + 9t$, find f when $a = 20$ and $t = 5$.
   c Given that $n = \dfrac{T}{5m}$ find n when $T = 240$ and $m = 8$.
   d Given that $P = 6d + 12e$, find P when $d = 13$ and $e = 15$.

2 The time, T seconds, for a person to travel n floors in a lift is given by the formula:

$$T = 10 + 7n$$

   a How long does it take to travel: **i** 3 floors, **ii** 19 floors, **iii** 1 floor?
   b i Calculate T when $n = 0$.
     ii What does your answer mean?

3 Isabelle mixes white and blue paint to make shades of blue. She uses this formula:

$$M = W + 25n$$

where M centilitres is the amount of mixed paint, W centilitres is the amount of white paint, n is the number of tins of blue paint.

   a How much paint does she get by mixing
     i 250 cl of white paint with 3 tins of blue paint
     ii 450 cl of white paint with 7 tins of blue paint.
   b i Calculate the value of M when $W = 0$ and $n = 1$.
     ii What does your answer mean?

4 N people equally share the cost of a meal. The amount, A, each person pays is given by the formula:

$$A = \dfrac{P + C - 20}{N}$$

where P pence is the cost of a pizza, and C pence is the cost of cola.

Calculate the amount each person pays if
   a 3 people buy a pizza costing 180p and cola costing 80p
   b 5 people buy a pizza costing £2.50 and cola costing £1.20.

5 The total length, L cm, of wool used by a group of n people who each knit s cm of a scarf is given by the formula:

$$L = 15ns$$

   a Calculate the total length of wool used when
     i 4 people each knit 43 cm
     ii 7 people each knit 22 cm.
   b How much wool does a 1 cm length of scarf contain?

1 Find the inverse of each function.

    a $x \to 6x$ **b** $x \to x + 7$ **c** $x \to \frac{x}{3}$ **d** $y = x - 1$

2 Find the inverse of each function.

    a $x \to 4x - 3$ **b** $x \to 10x + 2$ **c** $y = 2x - 4$ **d** $x \to \frac{x + 5}{3}$

3 **i** Find the function for each mapping diagram.
    ii Find the inverse of the function.

    a $x \to \Box$
        $1 \to 4$
        $2 \to 8$
        $3 \to 12$
        $4 \to 16$

    b $x \to \Box$
        $3 \to 6$
        $4 \to 7$
        $5 \to 8$
        $6 \to 9$

4 **a** Copy and complete the mapping diagram for the function $x \to 8 - x$.

    $x \to 8 - x$
    $1 \to \Box \to 1$
    $2 \to \Box \to 2$
    $3 \to \Box \to 3$
    $4 \to \Box \to 4$
    $x \to \Box$

    b Write down the inverse function.

Practice

3C Solving equations

Solve the following equations. Show your working.
Write each step on a new line.

1 **a** $4x = 24$ **b** $9x = 72$ **c** $7x = 49$ **d** $10w = 120$

2 **a** $\frac{x}{2} = 8$ **b** $\frac{x}{3} = 7$ **c** $\frac{x}{10} = 5$ **d** $\frac{a}{6} = 6$

3 **a** $x + 6 = 14$ **b** $x + 4 = 20$ **c** $x + 22 = 30$ **d** $k + 10 = 45$

4 **a** $x - 7 = 7$ **b** $x - 8 = 19$ **c** $x - 16 = 20$ **d** $i - 9 = 99$

5 **a** $3x + 7 = 13$ **b** $6x + 5 = 29$ **c** $10x - 17 = 73$ **d** $2y + 13 = 19$

6 **a** $2x - 3 = 11$ **b** $4x - 20 = 12$ **c** $3x - 6 = 15$ **d** $5v - 20 = 25$

7 **a** $4d = 44$ **b** $s - 5 = 10$ **c** $\frac{z}{4} = 9$ **d** $i + 12 = 21$
    e $3t + 8 = 23$ **f** $5m - 6 = 24$

3D Constructing equations to solve problems

For each question, write an equation and solve it.
Let x be the smaller unknown quantity.

1 Marcia has 13 more football cards than Derek. They have 89 cards altogether. How many does each person have?

Hint: Let x be the number of cards Derek has.

2 Warren bought both games for £79. How much does each game cost?

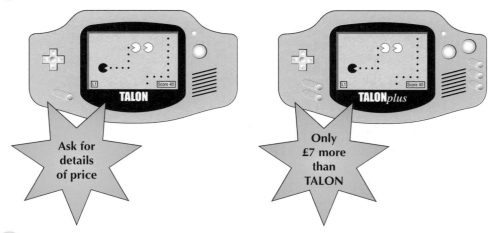

3 Michelle is three times my age. The sum of our ages is 36. How old am I?

4 A ExtraLight battery lasts four times as long as a Radiant battery. Both batteries last a total of 420 minutes. How long does each battery last?

5 Fahmida thought of a number, multiplied the number by three, then added 2. Her answer was 23. What was the number she first thought of?

3E Equations with unknown quantities on both sides

Solve the following equations.
Show your working.
Write each step on a new line.

1
  a $7x = 18 + x$
  b $5x = 9 + 2x$
  c $10y = 20 + 6y$
  d $9x = x + 40$
  e $8u = 3u + 35$
  f $7p = 3p + 32$

2
  a $3x = 20 - x$
  b $2x = 12 - 2x$
  c $4d = 30 - d$
  d $5p = 14 - 2p$

3
  a $5x + 4 = x + 16$
  b $6g + 5 = 2g + 13$
  c $9i + 7 = 5i + 19$
  d $4x - 3 = x + 9$
  e $10h - 3 = 3h + 18$
  f $8t - 15 = 6t - 3$

4
  a $9k = 35 + 2k$
  b $8i = 20 - 2i$
  c $7x + 3 = 2x + 23$
  d $5r - 10 = r + 18$
  e $5x = 3x + 8$
  f $4p - 15 = 3p - 12$

1 Daljit left a tap dripping. In 24 hours, 12 litres of water dripped from the tap.

    a Copy and complete the table.

Time (hours)	0	24
Water (litres)		

    b Plot the points on a graph and join them with a straight line.
Use the horizontal axis for up to 30 hours.
Use the vertical axis for up to 16 litres.
    c Use your graph to find the amount of water after
      i 5 hours   **ii** 10 hours   **iii** 27 hours.
    d Use your graph to find the time taken for the tap to drip
      i 7 litres   **ii** 10.5 litres   **iii** 14 litres.

2 £1 buys 7 Israeli shekels (NIS).

    a Copy and complete the table.

Pounds, £	0	20
Shekels, NIS		

    b Plot the points on a graph and join them with a straight line.
Use the horizontal axis for up to £20.
Use the vertical axis for up to 140 NIS.
    c Use your graph to convert these amounts to shekels.
      i £10   **ii** £17   **iii** £4
    d Use your graph to convert these amounts to pounds
      i 35 NIS   **ii** 77 NIS   **iii** 126 NIS

3 Harry sells cut-price CDs. The table shows some facts about his prices.

Number of CDs	0	20
Cost, £	0	90

    a Plot the points on a graph and join them with a straight line.
Use the horizontal axis for up to 20 CDs.
Use the vertical axis for up to £90.
    b Use your graph to find the cost of
      i 10 CDs   **ii** 18 CDs   **iii** 7 CDs.
    c Use your graph to find the number of CDs that can be bought for
      i £36   **ii** £63   **iii** £67.50.
    d Use the graph in question 2 to find the number of CDs that can be bought for 63 NIS.

Practice

4A Alternate and corresponding angles

1 Calculate the angles marked with letters. State whether you used alternate or corresponding angles.

a

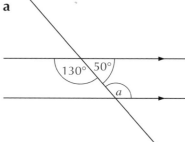

b

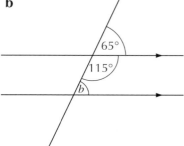

c

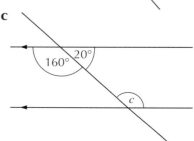

d

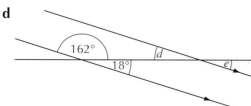

2 Calculate the angles marked with letters. Give a reason for each angle you find, i.e. alternate angles, corresponding angles or angles on a straight line.

a

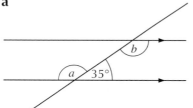

b

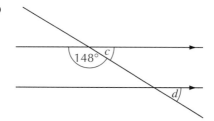

c

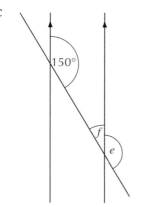

d

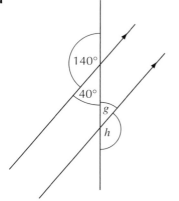

3 Calculate the angles marked with letters. Give a reason for each angle you calculate.

a

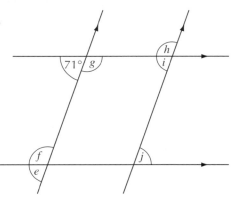

b

4B Angles of a triangle

1 Calculate the angles marked with letters.

a

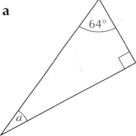

b

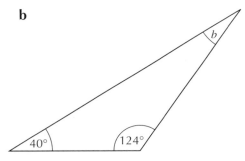

c

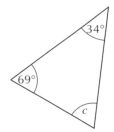

2 Calculate the angles marked with letters.

a

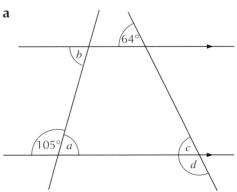

b

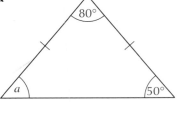

c

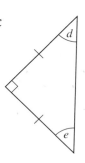

d

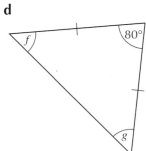

4

3 Calculate the angles marked with letters. Give a reason for each angle you find, i.e. angles on a straight line, angle sum of a triangle, isosceles triangle, equilateral triangle.

a

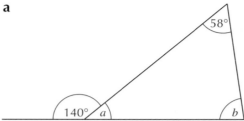

b

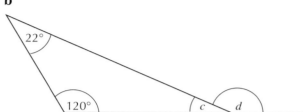

c

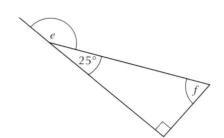

d

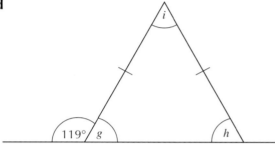

Practice

4C Angles of a quadrilateral

1 Calculate the angles marked with letters.

a

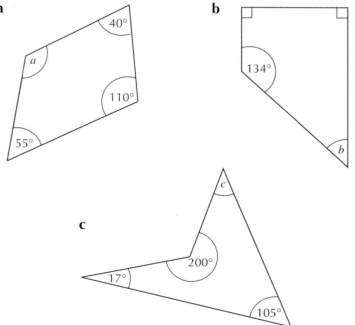

b

c

d

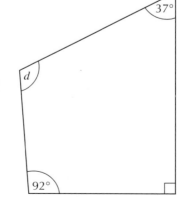

2 Calculate the angles marked with letters. Give a reason for each angle you find, i.e. angles on a straight line, angle sum of a quadrilateral.

a

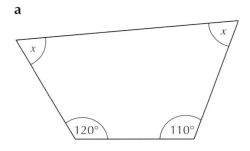

b

c

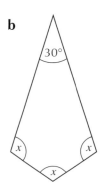

3 Find x.

a

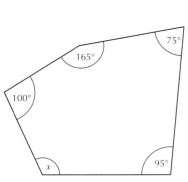

b

4D Interior angles of polygons

1 Calculate the size of the unknown interior angle.

a

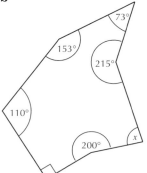

b

c

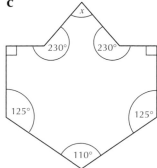

2 A regular nonagon has 9 sides.
   a How many triangles does this polygon contain?
   b What is the sum of its interior angles?
   c What is the size of each interior angle?

3 This regular polygon has 12 sides.

  a How many triangles does the polygon contain?

  b What is the sum of its interior angles?

  c What is the size of each interior angle?

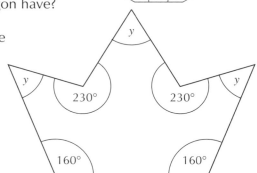

4 The sum of the interior angles of a polygon is 2520°.

  a How many triangles does the polygon contain?

  b How many sides does the polygon have?

5 The interior angles of a hexagon are 100°, 150°, 75°, 90°, 145° and x. Find x.

6 In the diagram on the right find interior angles y.

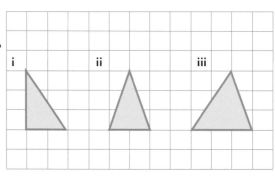

4E Tessellations

1 **a** Copy each triangle on to squared paper.
Does each triangle tessellate?

  b Draw a scalene triangle (three unequal sides) of your own on squared paper. Does it tessellate?

  c Does a triangle always tessellate? Explain your answer.

2 **a** Copy each quadrilateral on to squared paper. Does each quadrilateral tessellate?

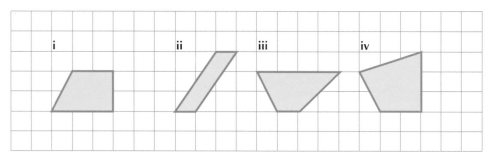

  b Draw a quadrilateral of your own on squared paper (not a special quadrilateral). Does it tessellate?

  c Does a quadrilateral always tessellate? Explain your answer.

1. Draw a line AB 13 cm long. Use a ruler and compasses to bisect the line. Check the bisection is correct using your ruler.

2. Repeat question 1 for a line AB 7.5 cm long.

3. Use a protractor to draw a 64° angle. Use a ruler and compasses to bisect the angle. Check the bisected angles using your protractor.

4. Repeat question 2 for the angle 134°.

5. Copy the kite using the following steps.
   - Draw a line AC 8 cm long.
   - Construct the perpendicular bisector of AC.
   - Use your ruler to mark points B and D.
   - Join up the points A, B, C and D.

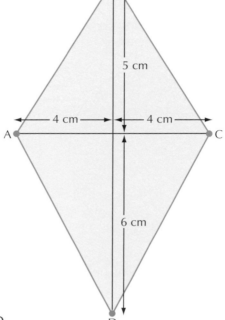

6. a Place your outstretched hand on a sheet of paper. Mark the end of your thumb, middle finger and little finger. Label the points A, B and C respectively.

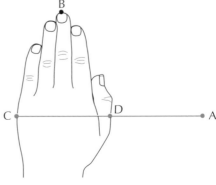

   b Draw the line AC. Bisect it using ruler and compasses. Label the midpoint D.
   c Compare the width of your closed hand to the length AD.

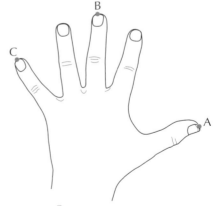

4G The circle and its parts

1 **a** Draw a circle with radius 33 mm.
    b Draw a circle with diameter 9.2 cm.
    c Draw a semicircle with diameter 8 cm.
    b Draw a quadrant of a circle with radius 52 cm.

2 Construct these diagrams.

Hint: To find out the radius of each circle, measure the diameter and halve it.

a

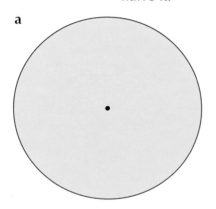

b

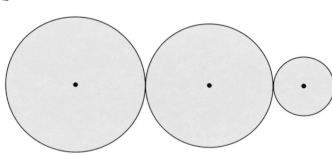

3 Construct these diagrams.

a

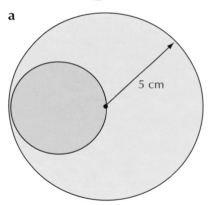

5 cm

b

3 cm

3 cm

c

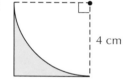

4 cm

4 **a** Draw a regular octagon.

Hint: Draw the circle first, then the diameters, then complete the polygon.

b Measure the length of the side of the polygon.

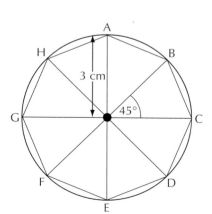

Handling Data 1

5A Pie charts

1 The table shows the type of floor covering in 40 dining rooms.
Draw a ten-sector pie chart of radius 6 cm.

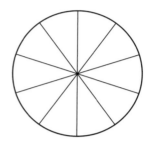

Floor covering	Wood	Carpet	Rug	Tiles
Number of rooms	16	12	8	4

2 The table shows the trees in an orchard.

Tree	Apple	Pear	Plum	Apricot	Cherry	Total
Number	22	14	10	10	4	60
Sector angle	132°					

a Copy and complete the table.   **b** Draw a circle with radius 6 cm.
c Draw a pie chart for the data.

3 Use the method in Q2 to draw pie charts for the following data.

a Books on a bookshelf.

Book	Novel	Textbook	Space	Sport	Total
Number	29	18	14	11	
Sector angle					

b Coins in a piggy bank.

Coin	1p	2p	5p	10p	20p	Total
Number	30	27	22	29	12	
Sector angle						

4 The pie chart shows the fish caught by a group of anglers. They caught 96 fish altogether.

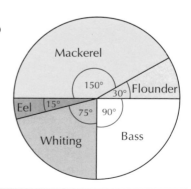

Copy and complete the table.

Fish	Mackerel	Flounder	Bass	Whiting	Eel
Number caught					

1 The graph shows the rates of unemployment over the last century.

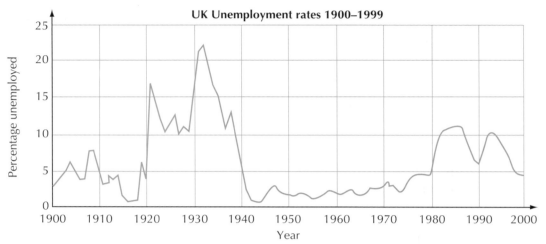

UK Unemployment rates 1900–1999

a In which decade was the rate of employment highest?

b Estimate the rate of unemployment in 1980.

c There were two periods when the rate of employment was close to zero. Why do you think there was little employment during these periods?

d Pierre says, 'Unemployment was about the same at the beginning of the century as at the end.' Is he correct?

2 People were asked to estimate the number of text messages they sent using their mobile phones during a month. The bar chart shows the results.

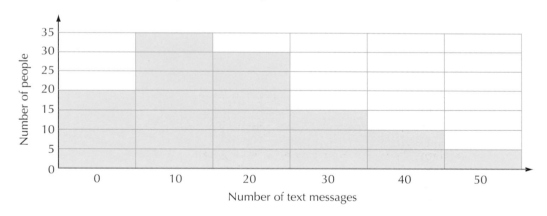

a Danielle says 'More than half the people do not send text messages.' Is she correct?

b Mervyn says 'More than twice as many people send 10 messages per month than 30 messages per month.' Is he correct?

c How many people were interviewed in the survey?

d 'Most people send 10 or 20 text messages per month.' Is this true?

e *Mobile Weekly* magazine claim that at least 25% of people send more than 30 text messages per month. Is this true?

f Write down two more observations based on the bar chart.

3 Chin Lin asked 20 people which instrument they prefer to listen to.
She drew this pie chart to show the results.

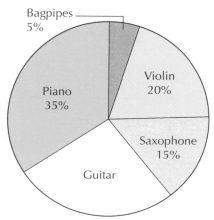

Favourite instrument

a Roughly a third of the people chose one of the instruments. Which one?

b What percentage of people chose the guitar?

c 'The violin is more popular than the bagpipes and saxophone combined.' Is this true?

d How many people chose the violin?

e Just over twice the number of people chose the piano as chose another instrument. Which other instrument?

f 'Stringed instruments are twice as popular as wind instruments.' Is this true? **Note:** stringed instruments include the piano.

g Write down two more comparisons based on the pie chart.

5C Two-way tables

1 The table shows details of the space launches during 2002.

		Country of launch		
		USA	Russia	Rest of the world
Purpose of launch	Communication satellite	8	9	10
	Other reason	10	16	11

a How many launches were from Russia?

b Joginder says, 'Most space launches are for communication satellites.' Is he correct?

c 'The USA and Russia launch more communication satellites than the rest of the world put together.' Is this true?

d How many launches were there in 2002?

e Write three more observations based on the table.

2 The tables show some holiday prices (£) to Tenerife and Gran Canaria.

Date	Tenerife			Gran Canaria		
	S/C	4*HB	A/I	S/C	4*HB	A/I
28 Feb	159	269	335	177	309	319
7 Mar	159	275	339	189	309	319
14 Mar	170	285	349	190	315	335
21 Mar	175	289	349	190	319	335
28 Mar	149	279	339	195	330	339
4 Apr	169	269	345	199	389	379

S/C = self-catering; 4*HB = 4-star hotel, half board; A/I = all-inclusive

a What is the most expensive holiday in March?
b What is the range of prices of holidays?
c Overall, from which date is it most expensive to travel to Tenerife?
d Describe any patterns you notice.
e Copy and complete the two-way table below showing the difference in price between holidays to Tenerife and Gran Canaria.

Date	Difference in price between Tenerife and Gran Canaria		
	S/C	4*HB	A/I
28 Feb			
7 Mar			
14 Mar			
21 Mar			
28 Mar			
4 Apr			

f Which type of holiday to Tenerife (S/C, 4*HB or A/I) varies in price the least? Explain your answer.

3 The table shows the percentages of people owning a computer in 1999 and 2002, and whether their computers were connected to the internet.

		1999		2002	
		Owns a computer connected to the internet	Owns a computer	Owns a computer connected to the internet	Owns a computer
Age	15–24	3	5	48	62
	25–34	14	47	51	61
	35–44	17	52	62	71
	45–54	15	48	53	61
	55–64	10	30	35	43
	65–74	4	15	13	20
	75+	2	7	7	10

Source for 2000 data: www.oftel.gov.uk/publications/research
Data for 1999 was estimated based on average percentage change from 2000.

a What percentage of people aged between 25 and 34 owned a computer connected to the internet in 2002?

b i What percentage of people between the ages of 15 and 54 owned a computer in 1999?

ii How does this compare with 2000?

c Make three more comparisons between 1999 and 2000.

d Harry says, 'The older a person gets, the less likely they are to own a computer.' Is he correct?

e In 1999, what percentage of people aged between 15 and 24 owned a computer that was *not* connected to the internet?

f Copy and complete the table below.

| | | Owns a computer that is *not* connected to the internet | |
		1999	**2002**
	15–24		
	25–34		
	35–44		
Age	45–54		
	55–64		
	65–74		
	75+		

Practice

5D Drawing and using frequency diagrams

1 For each frequency table, construct a frequency diagram.

a The table gives populations of villages without a shop.

Population, n	Number of villages
$0 < n - 100$	6
$100 < n - 200$	13
$200 < n - 300$	25
$300 < n - 400$	22
$400 < n - 500$	11

b The table gives the distance swum in a pool at a charity event.

Distance swum (d lengths)	Number of swimmers
$5 - d < 10$	18
$10 - d < 15$	15
$15 - d < 20$	11
$20 - d < 25$	7
$25 - d < 30$	2
$30 - d < 35$	1

c The table shows volumes (*V* cl) of liquid contained in 20 coconuts.

Volume of liquid (*V* cl)	Frequency
$10.0 \le V < 10.5$	2
$10.5 \le V < 11.0$	5
$11.0 \le V < 11.5$	3
$11.5 \le V < 12.0$	2
$12.0 \le V < 12.5$	4
$12.5 \le V < 13.0$	4

2 The durations (*t* minutes) of 30 telephone calls are shown below. Times have been rounded up to the nearest minute.

4	12	8	1	19	7	7	28	14	54
9	2	20	16	2	43	5	18	1	5
5	14	9	10	3	30	11	6	17	2

a Copy and complete the frequency table below.

Length of telephone call (*t* minutes)	Number of calls
$0 < \le £10$	
$10 < \le £20$	
$20 < \le £30$	
$30 < \le £40$	
$40 < \le £50$	
$50 < \le £60$	

b Draw a frequency diagram for the data.

3 The table shows the number of salmon caught at a fishing lodge during 1990.

Month	Feb	Mar	Apr	May	Jun	Jul	Aug	Sep
Number of salmon caught, *n*	20	60	20	30	70	30	50	100

a Draw a line graph for this data.
b During which month were most salmon caught?
c In which months were the same number of salmon caught?
d During which months were more than 40 salmon caught?
e What is the greatest difference in salmon caught from one month to the next?

Practice

5E A statistical investigation

Make two copies of the left column of the table on page 82 of Year 9
Pupil Book 1.
Use the information in the two accounts below to complete the right column
in each table.

1 Tania is investigating our sense of balance. She decides to time how long
people can balance objects. She decides to concentrate on balancing a
ruler on end. She thinks that longer rulers are easier to balance, and that
one hand will be better than the other.

2 Darryl is investigating the relationship between diet and exercise. He thinks
that vegetarians exercise more than non-vegetarians. He decides to ask
people if they are vegetarian and how much they exercise each week.
He needs to find enough vegetarians to interview; luckily there is a
vegetarian cafe in town.

CHAPTER 6 Shape, Space and Measures 2

Practice

6A Area of a triangle

1 Calculate the areas of the following triangles.

a

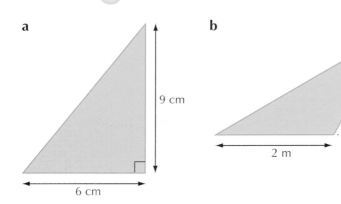

9 cm

6 cm

b

2 m

2 m

c

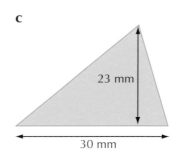

23 mm

30 mm

d

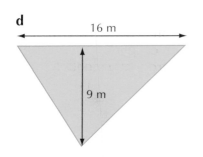

16 m

9 m

e

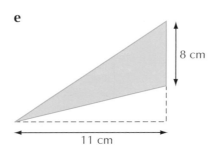

8 cm

11 cm

f

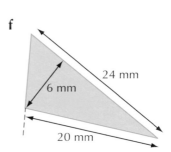

24 mm

6 mm

20 mm

2 Copy and complete the table which gives the measurements of five triangles.

Base	Height	Area
12 cm	9 cm	
8 cm	14 cm	
6 mm	7 mm	
16 cm		64 cm^2
	20 m	100 m^2

3 Use squared paper to draw four different triangles with area 24 cm^2.

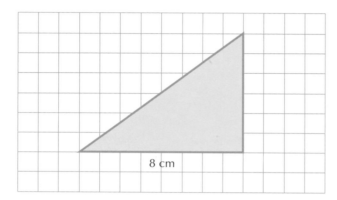

8 cm

Hint: Draw the base first, using a whole number of centimetres that is a factor of 48, e.g. 8 cm, as shown in the example. Then calculate the height of the triangle.

4 Find the area of each compound shape.

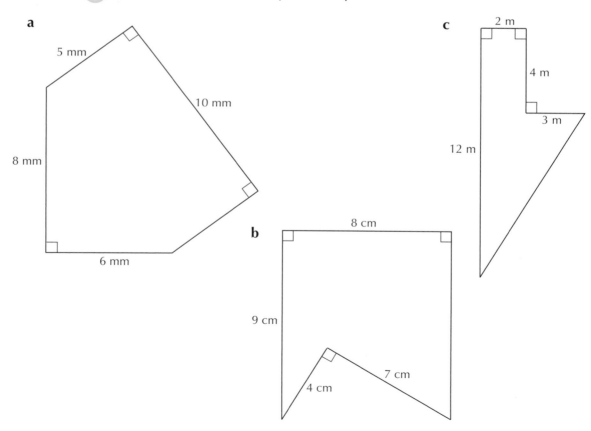

a

5 mm

10 mm

8 mm

6 mm

b

8 cm

9 cm

4 cm

7 cm

c

2 m

4 m

3 m

12 m

5 Find the area of each shape.

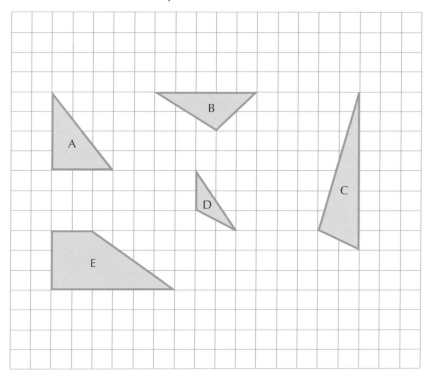

6B Area of a parallelogram and area of a trapezium

1 Calculate the areas of the following parallelograms.

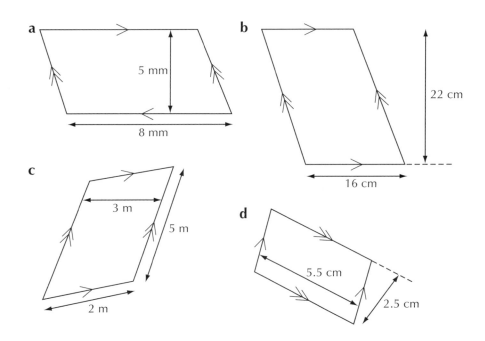

a 5 mm, 8 mm

b 22 cm, 16 cm

c 3 m, 5 m, 2 m

d 5.5 cm, 2.5 cm

2 Copy and complete the table below which gives the measurements of five parallelograms.

Base	Height	Area
7 cm	13 cm	
9 m	19 m	
250 mm	70 mm	
	15 m	120 m^2
12 cm		30 cm^2

3 Use squared paper to draw four different parallelograms with area 48 cm^2.

Hint: Draw the base first (a whole number of centimetres that is a factor of 48, e.g. 8 cm). Then calculate the height of the parallelogram.

4 Calculate the areas of the trapezia below.

a

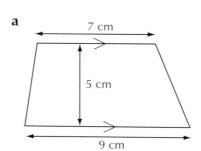

7 cm

5 cm

9 cm

b

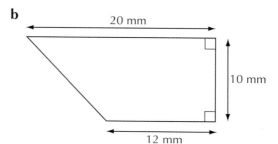

20 mm

10 mm

12 mm

c

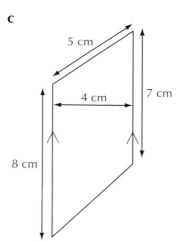

5 cm

4 cm

7 cm

8 cm

d

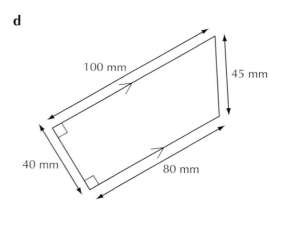

100 mm

45 mm

40 mm

80 mm

5 Copy and complete the table for trapezia **a** to **e**.

Trapezium	Parallel side a	Parallel side b	Height h	Area
a	7 cm	9 cm	3 cm	
b	13 m	8 m	5 m	
c	2 mm	6 mm		32 mm^2
d		4 m	6 m	60 m^2
e	12 cm		10 cm	250 cm^2

6C Volume of a cuboid

1 Calculate the volume of each cuboid.

a

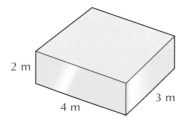

2 m, 4 m, 3 m

b

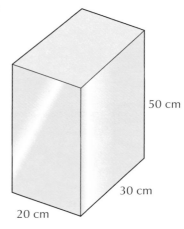

50 cm, 30 cm, 20 cm

c

6 cm, 6 cm, 125 cm

2 Calculate the capacity of each cuboid in question 1.

3 Calculate the volume and capacity of a cube of side **a** 20 cm, **b** 3 m.

4 Calculate the capacity of a fish tank with dimensions 60 cm by 30 cm by 20 cm.

5 Copy and complete the table for cuboids **a** to **d**.

Cuboid	Length, l	Width, w	Height, h	Volume, V	Capacity
a	10 cm	40 cm	5 cm		
b	2 m	7 m	9 m		
c	5 cm	16 cm		4000 cm^3	
d		10 cm	25 cm	3500 cm^3	

6 Krispies are sold in three sizes: mini, medium and giant. The boxes are filled to the top.

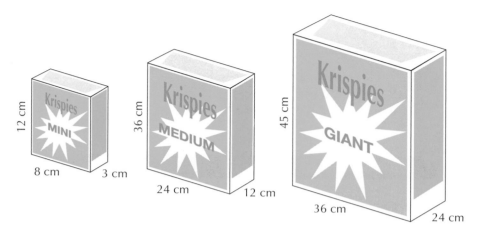

a Calculate the volume of each box.
b How many times bigger is the giant box compared to the medium box?
c How many mini boxes could be fitted into:
  i a medium box
  ii a giant box?

Practice

6D Imperial units

1 Convert each of the following quantities to the units shown in brackets.

a 7 yd (ft)   b 6 ft (in)   c 9 ft 7 in (in)
d 5 ft 11(in)   e 7 miles (yd)   f 5 st (lb)
g 3 st 6 lb   h $3\frac{1}{2}$ ton (lb)   i 4 gal (pt)
j $3\frac{1}{4}$ gallons (pt)

2 Convert each of the following quantities to the units shown in brackets.

a 48 in (ft)   b 55 in (ft and in)   c 64 oz (lb)
d 83 oz (lb and oz)   e 54 ft (yd)   f 70 ft (yd and ft)
g 40 pt (gal)   h 75 pt (gal and pt)   i 60 lb (st and lb)
j 123 in (yd, ft and in)

3 a How many stones are in a ton?
   b How many feet are in a mile?

4 Convert each Imperial quantity to the approximate metric quantity shown in brackets.

a 11 oz (g)   b 35 miles (km)   c 100 in (cm)
d 2 lb (g)   e 21 pt (l)   f 154 yd (m)
g 3 lb 12 oz (g)   h 1 ft 4 in (cm)

5 Calculate the approximate length of this tape measure in metres.

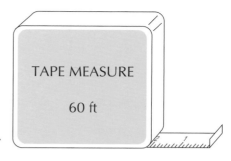

TAPE MEASURE

60 ft

6 **a** A barrel of ale holds 288 pints. How many gallons does it hold?

b A hogshead of wine holds 63 gallons. How many pints does it hold?

7 Convert this biscuit recipe to metric units.

8 You know that 1 in is about 2.5 cm and 1 oz is about 30 g. Find a close metric approximation (shown in brackets) for each of the following.

a 1 yd (cm) **b** 1 lb (g) **c** 1 mile (m)

Biscuits

1lb 9oz	plain flour
12oz	butter
$7\frac{1}{2}$oz	sugar
2oz	rice flour
$\frac{1}{2}$oz	salt

Practice

6E Finding the mid-point of a line segment

1 Copy the grid and plot the points.

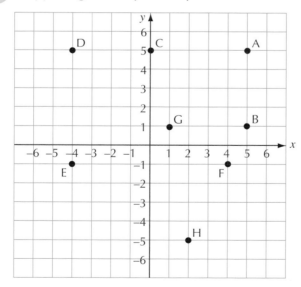

a Make a list of the coordinates of the points.

b Copy the diagram.

c Join these pairs of points using straight lines.

i AB **ii** AD **iii** DE

iv EF **v** BG **vi** AG **vii** EH

d Find the mid-point of each line in part **c**.

2 Copy the grid and plot the points.

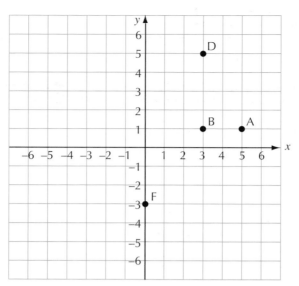

a Find the mid-point of the lines
    i AB   **ii** BD   **iii** AD
b B is the mid-point of line AC.
    Find the coordinates of point C and plot it.
c B is the mid-point of line DE.
    Find the coordinates of point E and plot it.
d F is the mid-point of line EG.
    Find the coordinates of point G and plot it.

Practice

7A Powers of 10

1 Multiply these numbers by **i** 10^2 and **ii** 10^3.

   a 0.42   **b** 874   **c** 12.6   **d** 0.053   **e** 0.0004

2 Divide these numbers by **i** 10 and **ii** 10^2.

   a 4300   **b** 0.6   **c** 23.7   **d** 0.054   **e** 13 599

3 Multiply these numbers by **i** 0.01 and **ii** 0.1.

   a 600   **b** 5   **c** 23 000   **d** 0.6   **e** 25.2

4 Divide these numbers by **i** 0.1 and **ii** 0.01.

   a 7   **b** 0.54   **c** 98
   d 0.012   **e** 492   **f** 0.0087

5 Calculate these numbers.

   a 5.25×10^3 **b** $0.43 \div 0.01$
   c $7450 \div 10^2$ **d** 25×0.01
   e 0.003×10^2 **f** $63 \div 0.1$
   g $0.72 \div 10$ **h** 0.056×10^3

6 Copy and complete each ladder of calculations.

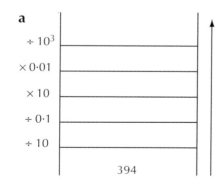
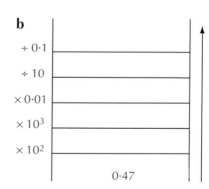

Practice

7B Rounding

1 Round these numbers **i** to 1 decimal place and **ii** to 2 decimal places.

   a 2.874   **b** 0.05537   **c** 20.957   **d** 0.5059   **e** 9.98407

2 Round these numbers to one significant figure.

   a 327   **b** 8.452   **c** 8175   **d** 0.06594   **e** 79 550
   f 0.007 29   **g** 20.981

3 Estimate answers to these by first rounding the numbers to 1 significant figure.

a 7.6×47 b 12% of $2761
c $3897 \div 97$ d $5.38 \times (13.85 - 4.199)$
e $3.54^2 - 2.22^2$ f $916.7 \div 2.86$
g $\dfrac{5.018 \times 3.86}{11.41 - 6.459}$ h $\dfrac{37.71 + 18.099}{8.29 - 3.33}$

4 Round these quantities to an appropriate degree of accuracy.

a Jeremy is 1.8256 m tall.
b A computer disk holds 688 332 800 bytes of information.
c A petrol tank has a capacity of 72.892 litres.
d An English dictionary contains 59 238 722 words.
e Kailash held his breath for 82.71 seconds.

5 Use a calculator to work out these numbers.
Round your answers to a suitable degree of accuracy.

a 7392^2 b $\dfrac{5}{7}$

c $18.3 + 2.8 \times 9.7 \times 1.4$ d $\dfrac{997 - 285}{0.863 \times 5.25}$

Practice

7C Recurring decimals

1 Calculate these fractions as decimals. Describe each answer as a terminating or recurring decimal.

a $\dfrac{17}{30}$ b $\dfrac{7}{8}$ c $\dfrac{27}{50}$ d $\dfrac{9}{70}$ e $\dfrac{15}{22}$

2 Write these fractions as recurring decimals.

a $\dfrac{5}{9}$ b $\dfrac{1}{6}$ c $\dfrac{8}{11}$

d $\dfrac{100}{909}$ e $\dfrac{7}{90}$ f $\dfrac{148}{990}$

3 a Copy and complete these recurring decimals.

$\dfrac{1}{33} = 0.\overset{\bullet\bullet}{03}$

$\dfrac{2}{33} =$

......

$\dfrac{12}{33} =$

$\dfrac{13}{33} =$

b Describe how to write any 'thirty-third' as a recurring decimal without using a calculator, e.g. $\dfrac{15}{33}$.

4 Do not use a calculator for this question.

$$\frac{2}{3} = 0.666\ 666\ ...$$

$$\frac{2}{30} = 0.066\ 666\ ...$$

$$\frac{2}{300} = 0.006\ 666\ ...$$

  a Write down the recurring decimal for $\frac{2}{3000}$.

  b Use your answers to question 2 to write recurring decimals for these fractions.

    i $\frac{5}{90}$ **ii** $\frac{5}{900}$ **iii** $\frac{1}{60}$

    iv $\frac{1}{600}$ **v** $\frac{8}{110}$ **vi** $\frac{8}{1100}$

Practice

7D Multiplying decimals

Do not use a calculator. Show your working.

1 **a** 0.4×0.2 **b** 0.04×0.2 **c** 0.7×0.6 **d** 0.7×0.06
    e 0.09×0.9 **f** 0.9×0.9 **g** 0.04×0.3 **h** 0.8×0.03

2 **a** 300×0.7 **b** 0.2×70 **c** 80×0.5 **d** 0.7×800
    e 400×0.01 **f** 0.06×500 **g** 2000×0.03 **h** 0.002×6000

3 **a** 7×2.6 **b** 0.8×7.1 **c** 5.51×0.2 **d** 0.3×9.25

4 Rice costs £2.15 per kg. Calculate the cost of 0.8 kg of rice. Work in £.

5 The tank of a model aeroplane holds 8.28 cl of fuel. How much fuel is needed to fill the tank 6 times?

Practice

7E Dividing decimals

Do not use a calculator. Show your working.

1 **a** $0.84 \div 0.2$ **b** $0.49 \div 0.7$ **c** $0.24 \div 0.8$ **d** $0.66 \div 0.1$

2 **a** $50 \div 0.2$ **b** $200 \div 0.8$ **c** $30 \div 0.6$ **d** $900 \div 0.3$

3 **a** $5.2 \div 4$ **b** $2.8 \div 70$ **c** $72 \div 80$ **d** $9.6 \div 60$

4 **a** $6.4 \div 32$ **b** $5.5 \div 2.5$ **c** $2.7 \div 1.8$ **d** $25.5 \div 3.4$

5 30 buttons cost 228p. Calculate the cost of one button.

6 How many stamps fit across the top of the envelope?

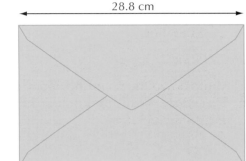

28.8 cm

26p

1.8 cm

7F Efficient use of a calculator

Round your answers to a suitable degree of accuracy, where necessary.

1 Use the power key on your calculator to evaluate these numbers.

  a 6^6 **b** 0.81^3 **c** 1.272 **d** 230^3

2 Use the fraction key to calculate these.

  a $\frac{7}{10} + \frac{9}{20} - \frac{3}{5}$ **b** $2\frac{1}{3} \div 1\frac{8}{9}$ **c** $\frac{3}{5} \times \left(\frac{7}{9} - \frac{2}{3}\right)$ **d** $\left(3\frac{2}{3}\right)^2$

3 Calculate these.

  a $2.5^2 \times (1.8 + 5.4)$ **b** $3^3 - 2.5^2$

  c $(12^3 + 17 + 25) \div 30$ **d** $\sqrt{0.9^2 + 0.6^2}$

  e $\sqrt{13 - \frac{7}{11}}$

4 Calculate the perimeter of the dinner mat.

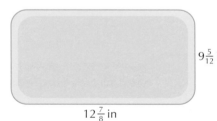

$9\frac{5}{12}$ in

$12\frac{7}{8}$ in

5 **a** Press these keys on your calculator.

  i $\boxed{1}\ \boxed{x!}\ \boxed{=}$

  ii $\boxed{2}\ \boxed{x!}\ \boxed{=}$

  iii $\boxed{3}\ \boxed{x!}\ \boxed{=}$

  b Copy and complete this table.

x	1	2	3	4	5
$x!$					

  c Describe any pattern you notice.

  d Use your pattern to find the answer to $\boxed{6}\ \boxed{x!}\ \boxed{=}$
Check your answer using a calculator.

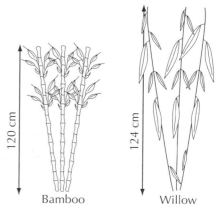

e Copy and complete these calculations.

$1 = 1$
$2 \times 1 = 2$
$3 \times 2 \times 1 =$
$4 \times 3 \times 2 \times 1 =$

f What do you notice about the answers?

g Use $\boxed{x!}$ to calculate:

i $9 \times 8 \times 7 \times 6 \times 5 \times 4 \times 3 \times 2 \times 1$

ii $12 \times 11 \times 10 \times 9 \times 8 \times 7 \times 6 \times 5 \times 4 \times 3 \times 2 \times 1$

Practice

7G Solving problems

1 Jonathan has been on a diet. He wants to weigh less than 70 kg.
He used some old weighing scales and found his weight was 155 lb.
Does he need to stay on the diet? Use the conversion: 1 kg = 2.2 lb.

2 Which biscuit purchase gives the best value? Explain your answer.

a

Crumblies
BISCUITS
74p
20 biscuits

b

Crumblies *extra value*
BISCUITS
£1.19
35 biscuits

c

Crumblies
BISCUITS
£1.26
Family Pack
36 biscuits

3 The total capacity of 5 cups and 3 mugs is 230 cl.
The total capacity of 5 cups and 4 mugs is 265 cl.

a Find the capacity of a mug.
b Find the capacity of a cup.

4 Arooma thinks of a number, adds 4 then doubles the result.
Her answer is 42.
What was the number she first thought of?

5 The diagram shows the heights of two trees. During the next year, the bamboo tree grew 10% and the willow tree grew 5%. Which is the taller tree now?

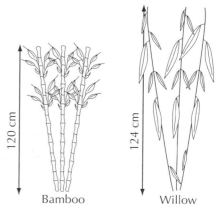

120 cm — Bamboo

124 cm — Willow

6 The TV programme Wacko Magic lasts 25 minutes and is shown every Tuesday and Thursday.
Country Facts lasts 15 minutes and is shown every Wednesday.
Karen records these programmes each week. She has recorded 7 hours and 35 minutes on a videotape.

a How many weeks did she record?
b How many of each programme did she record?

CHAPTER **8** Algebra 4

8A HCF and LCM

1 Write down the first ten multiples of each number.

    a 4   **b** 6   **c** 9   **d** 10   **e** 15

2 Use your answers to question 1 to find the LCM of these numbers.

    a 4 and 6   **b** 6 and 9   **c** 4 and 10   **d** 6 and 15   **e** 9 and 15

3 Which numbers in the cloud are multiples of **a** 7, **b** 12 and **c** 16?

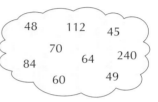

48   112   45   70   64   240   84   60   49

4 List all the factors of each number.

    a 8   **b** 18   **c** 28
    d 42   **e** 63   **f** 100

5 Use your answers to question 4 to find the HCF of:

    a 8 and 18   **b** 18 and 42   **c** 28 and 63
    d 18 and 63   **e** 42 and 63   **f** 28 and 100

6 Find the LCM of each pair of numbers.

    a 3 and 10   **b** 8 and 10   **c** 6 and 12   **d** 9 and 21   **e** 16 and 24

7 Find the HCF of each pair of numbers.

    a 20 and 30   **b** 18 and 30   **c** 12 and 36   **d** 15 and 25   **e** 36 and 90

8 **a** Write down a pair of numbers with an HCF of 6.
     b Write down a pair of numbers with an LCM of 50.

8B Powers and roots

Do not use a calculator for the first 6 questions. Show your working.

1 Calculate these numbers.

    a 13^2 **b** 20^2 **c** 11^3
    d 30^3 **e** $6^2 + 3^3$ **f** $9^3 - 8^2$

2 Calculate these numbers.

    a $\sqrt{121}$ **b** $\sqrt{169}$ **c** $\sqrt{10\,000}$ **d** $\sqrt[3]{729}$
    e $\sqrt{16} + 5^3$ **f** $4^2 - \sqrt[3]{1}$ **g** $\sqrt{81} - \sqrt[3]{512}$ **h** $\sqrt[3]{0}$

3 Find the positive value of x that makes each equation true.

   a $x^2 = 4$ **b** $x^2 = 144$

4 Find the missing area or side for each square.

  a   **b**   **c**   **d**

5 Find the missing volume or side for each cube.

 a   **b**   **c**   **d**

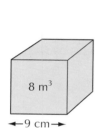
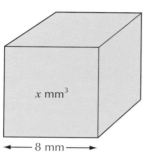
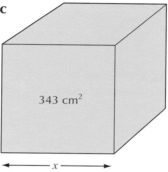
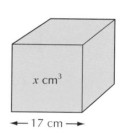

6 **a** Explain how you can tell that $\sqrt{70}$ is between 8 and 9.
    b Which two whole numbers are closest to $\sqrt{120}$?
    c Explain how you can tell that $\sqrt[3]{500}$ is between 7 and 8.
    d Which two whole numbers are closest to $\sqrt[3]{7}$?

7 Calculate these, giving your answers correct to 1 decimal place.

   a 231^2 **b** 25^3 **c** $\sqrt{7}$

   d $\sqrt{5000}$ **e** $\sqrt[3]{2}$ **f** $\sqrt[3]{78\,000}$

Practice

8C Prime factors

1 Find the number that these prime factors give.

   a $3 \times 3 \times 11$ **b** $7 \times 7 \times 13$ **c** $2 \times 2 \times 5 \times 7$ **d** $2 \times 2 \times 2 \times 2 \times 3$

2 Find the number that these prime factors give.

   a $3^2 \times 7$ **b** $2^3 \times 5^2$ **c** $3 \times 5 \times 7^2$ **d** $2^2 \times 3 \times 5^3$

3 Use a prime factor tree to find the prime factors of each number.
Write your answers using powers, where possible.

   a 18   **b** 55   **c** 27   **d** 72   **e** 60

4 Use the division method to find the prime factors of each number. Write your answers using powers, where possible.

    a 84   **b** 100   **c** 175   **d** 156   **e** 224

5 Write down the common prime factors for eah pair of numbers. Find the HCF and LCM for each pair.

    a $48 = 2 \times 2 \times 2 \times 2 \times 3$ **b** $110 = 2 \times 5 \times 11$
       $54 = 2 \times 3 \times 3 \times 3$ $200 = 2 \times 2 \times 2 \times 5 \times 5$

6 Use prime factors to find the HCF of each pair of numbers.

    a 20 and 28   **b** 30 and 36   **c** 42 and 70

7 Use prime factors to find the LCM of each pair of numbers.

    a 8 and 12   **b** 15 and 20   **c** 18 and 30

8 Use prime factors to find the HCF and LCM for each pair of numbers.

    a 40 and 50   **b** 66 and 90   **c** 150 and 175

Practice

8D Graphs of the form $y = mx + c$

1 Write down the value of m and c in these equations of straight lines.

    a $y = 4x + 2$ **b** $y = 0.5x - 1$ **c** $y = 7$
    d $y = 7x$ **e** $y = x$

2 Write down the equation of a straight line given these values of m and c.

    a $m = 2, c = 4$ **b** $m = \frac{1}{4}, c = 1$ **c** $m = 10, c = -2$
    d $m = 0, c = -3$ **e** $m = 3, c = 0$ **f** $m = -1, c = 0$

3 **a** Copy and complete the table for the equations of straight lines.

x	0	1	2	3
$y = 2x$				
$y = 2x - 1$				
$y = 2x - 2$				
$y = 2x - 3$	-3			

    b Draw a grid with x-axis from 0 to 3 and y-axis from -5 to 6.
    c Draw a straight-line graph for each equation.
    d What do you notice about the lines?
    e Sketch these lines without calculating any coordinates.
       i $y = 2x - 4$ **ii** $y = 2x - 1.5$
    f Suppose you draw the graph of $y = 2x - c$, where c is any positive number. What can you say about the graph?

4 **a** Copy and complete the table for the equations of straight lines.

x	0	1	2	3
$y = -x$		−1		
$y = -2x$				
$y = -3x$				
$y = -4x$				−12

b Draw a grid with x-axis from 0 to 3 and y-axis from −15 to 0.
c Draw a straight-line graph for each equation.
d What do you notice about the lines?
e Sketch these lines without calculating any coordinates.
   i $y = -5x$ **ii** $y = -2.5x$
f Suppose you draw the graph of $y = -mx$, where m is any positive number. What can you say about the graph?

CHAPTER 9 Handling Data 2

Practice

9A Mutually exclusive events

1 The diagram shows 8 faces printed on badges.
The badges are placed in a bag. One is chosen at random from the bag.
Which of these pairs of events are mutually exclusive?
Note: 'Left eye' means the eye on the left of the diagram.

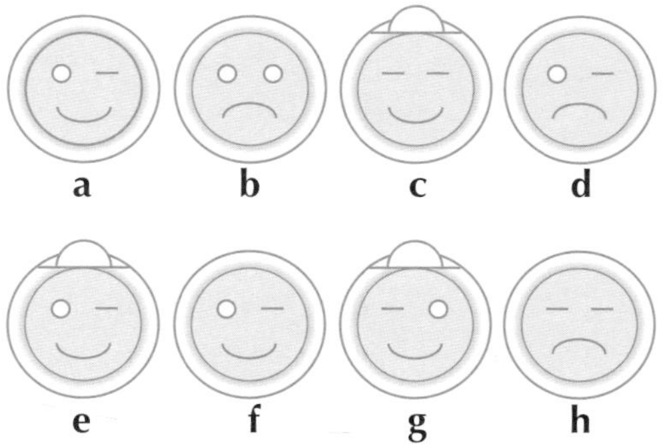

a   b   c   d
e   f   g   h

a A smiling face. A sad face.
b Left eye shut. Both eyes shut.
c Wearing a hat. Both eyes open.
d Both eyes open. A sad face.
e Wearing a hat. Right eye shut.
f Smiling with an eye open. Right eye shut.

2 A six-sided dice is numbered 1, 2, 3, 3, 4, 6. It is rolled once.
Here are some events.

A number 3   **B** even number
C number greater than 3   **D** square number
E multiple of 3   **F** number less than 5

a Write down three pairs of events that are mutually exclusive.
b Write down three pairs of events that are *not* mutually exclusive.

3 The dice is rolled and the spinner is spun.

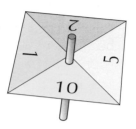

The number on the dice is divided by the number on the spinner.
Copy and complete the table of outcomes.

		Dice					
		1	**2**	**3**	**4**	**5**	**6**
Spinner	**1**						
	2						
	5						
	10						

9B Calculating probabilities

1 The letters of the word SUCCESSOR are written on cards and placed in a bag. One of the cards is withdrawn from the bag. Work out the probability that the letter is:

a S
b a vowel
c one of the last 10 letters of the alphabet
d a C or an S
e a consonant
f a letter of the word ROSE.

2 The names of two children, KIM and FRANZ, are written on cards and placed in a bag. These coins are placed in the same bag: 1p, 2p, 5p, 10p, 20p, 50p, £1. A card and a coin are taken from the bag at random. The coin is given to the person on the card.

a Copy and complete the list of possible outcomes as:
KIM, 1p
KIM, 2p
......

b Calculate the probability that:
i Kim receives 20p
ii Franz receives less than 10p
iii one of the children receives 10p
iv Kim does not receive £1
v neither child receives more than 20p.

3 A taxi firm owns a red and a green taxi cab. The red taxi can carry up to six passengers. The green taxi can carry up to five passengers.

a Copy and complete the table showing the total number of passengers being carried at any one time.

		Red taxi		
		1	**2**	**3**
	1	2		
Green taxi	**2**			
	3			6

b Work out the probability that, at any one time, the number of passengers being carried is:

i 7	**ii** 2	**iii** 12
iv less than 5	**v** an odd number	**vi** 2 or 7

9C Estimates of probability

1 Charlie flipped a coin 80 times and obtained 56 heads.

a Estimate the probability of flipping heads next time.
b Do you think the coin is fair? Explain your answer.

2 These five identical buttons were dropped 50 times.

The number of buttons that fell white side up was recorded each time. The table summarises the results.

Number of buttons falling white side up	0	1	2	3	4	5
Frequency	1	11	17	15	4	2
Relative frequency		0.22				

a Copy and complete the table.
b Estimate the estimated probability of:
   i 3 buttons falling white side up
   ii no buttons falling white side up
   iii more than 3 buttons falling white side up.

3 A company that manufactures computer chips makes regular quality control checks. The table shows how many computer chips are checked and how many of them are faulty.

	Hourly check	Daily check	Weekly check	Monthly check
Number of chips checked	20	50	200	500
Number of chips faulty	3	8	26	72
Relative frequency				

  a Copy and complete the table.
  b Estimate the probability of a computer chip being faulty. Choose your best estimate.

CHAPTER 10 Shape, Space and Measures 3

Practice

10A Enlargements

1 Trace each shape with its centre of enlargement O. Enlarge the shape by the given scale factor.

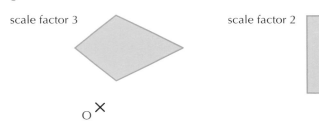

scale factor 3

scale factor 2

2 a Copy the grid and shape A only. Enlarge shape A by a scale factor of 2, using the origin as centre of enlargement. Label the image A'.

b Copy the grid and shape B only. Enlarge shape B by a scale factor of 2, using point (7, 10) as centre of enlargement. Label the image B'.

c Copy the grid and shape C only. Enlarge shape C by a scale factor of 3, using point (5, 4) as centre of enlargement. Label the image C'.

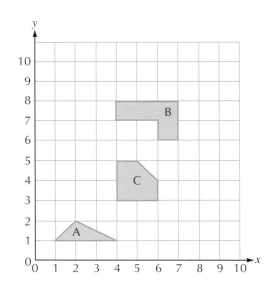

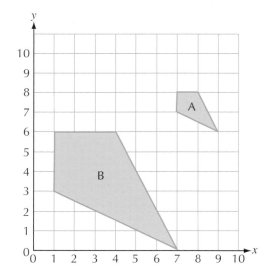

3 **a** Copy the diagram.
   b Shape B is an enlargement of shape A. What is the scale factor?
   c Draw ray lines to find the centre of enlargement. Write down the coordinates of this point.

10B 3-D symmetry

1 Which of these objects have reflective symmetry?

   a electric light bulb   **b** shoe   **c** playground roundabout

2 Write down the number of planes of symmetry each shape has.

a
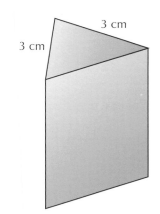

b
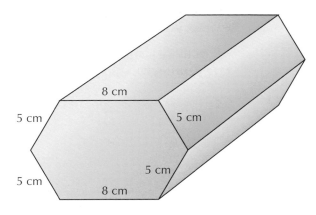

3 Sketch each shape. Draw a plane of symmetry using dotted lines or shading. Make a copy of the shape for every plane of symmetry.

a
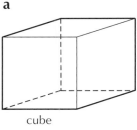
cube

b
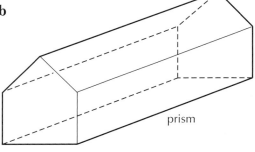
prism

c
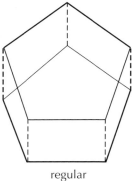
regular pentagon

4 Copy each shape using an isometric grid. Draw a plane of symmetry using dotted lines or shading. Make a copy of the shape for every plane of symmetry.

a

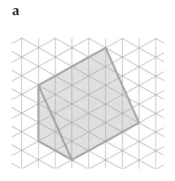

b

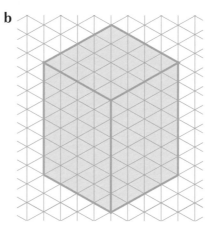

c

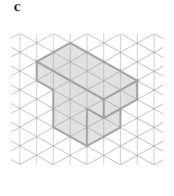

5 Sketch a different solid with exactly one plane of symmetry. Use a dotted line to show the plane of symmetry.

10C Scale drawings

All of these shapes are drawn to scale.
Use centimetre squared paper for all drawings.

1 Measure the sides of each shape and draw to its actual size.

c

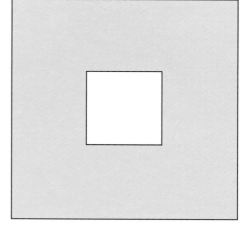

a

b

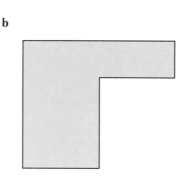

Scale: 1 cm to 2 cm   Scale: 1 cm to 3 cm   Scale: 1 cm to 2.5 cm

2 Measure the horizontal and vertical sides of each shape and draw to its actual size. Measure the length of the sloping side of your drawing.

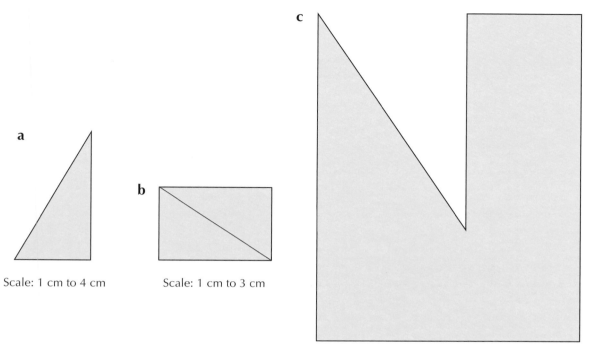

a

Scale: 1 cm to 4 cm

b

Scale: 1 cm to 3 cm

c

Scale: 1 cm to 2.5 cm

3 This is the plan of an indoor kite. Measure the horizontal and vertical lines. Draw the kite to its actual size. Measure the lengths of the sides and mark them on your diagram.

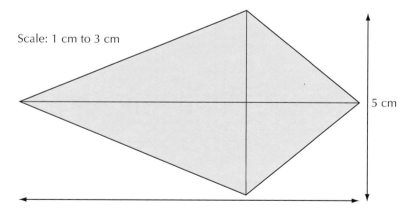

Scale: 1 cm to 3 cm

5 cm

CHAPTER 11 Algebra 5

11A Like terms and simplification

Simplify these expressions.

1
a $5y + 3y$ b $8i + 4i$ c $9p - 2p$ d $4t - t$
e $3n - 5n$ f $a - 4a$ g $-5g + 7g$ h $-7h + 2h$
i $-3u - 4u$ j $-t - 7t$

2
a $2m + 5m + 3m$ b $x + 2x + 3x + 4x$ c $8c - 2c + 3c$
d $10d - 3d - 5d$ e $4p + p - 2p$ f $7t - 2t - 9t$

3
a $3v + 2v + s$ b $9r - 3r - 3$ c $5t + 5d - 2d$
d $4f + 3g + 2f$ e $9n - 2p - 5n$ f $7 + 2u - 8u$

4
a $4e + 3e + 2u + 6u$ b $5k - 2k + 3h - 7h$
c $3y + 2x + 2y + 4x$ d $5s + 2t - 3s - t$
e $7y + 4k - 2k - 3y$ f $3i + 4h - 6i + 2h$
g $7m - 9c - 3m + 2c$ h $-j + 4l + 3j - 6l$

5 A measuring cup contains x grams of flour when full.
It is used to make these piles of flour.

| $5x + 20$ | $3x$ | $100 - 2x$ | $200 - x$ |
| A | B | C | D |

a Calculate the total weight of:
  i piles A and B   ii piles B and D
  iii piles C and D   iv all the piles of flour.
b How much more flour is there in pile A than pile B?

11B Expanding brackets

Expand the brackets.

1
a $5(d + 2)$ b $7(2p - 1)$ c $4(3 + m)$ d $10(5 - 3i)$

2
a $-6(3a + 2)$ b $-4(2H - 6)$ c $-2(2w + 3)$ d $-6(5 - 6x)$

3
a $c(d - 7)$ b $m(5 + n)$ c $d(e + f)$ d $w(i - k)$
e $t(3h - 1)$ f $u(4 - 5v)$ g $-a(b + 3)$ h $-h(3 - m)$

4 a $m(m + 1)$ **b** $u(4 - u)$ **c** $p(2p + 3)$ **d** $x(5 - 2x)$
   e $i(3i + 2)$ **f** $-d(2d - 3)$ **g** $-y(x - y)$ **h** $-h(h + 1)$

5 An envelope costs 5 pence and a stamp costs s pence.
   a Write down an expression for the cost of:
     i a stamped envelope
     ii 6 stamped envelopes
     iii n stamped envelopes.
   b Expand the brackets for your answers to parts **ii** and **iii**.

6 A box contains b grams of salt. The box weighs 10 g.
   a Write down an expression for the total weight of these.
     i a box of salt
     ii 3 boxes of salt
     iii m boxes of salt.
   b Expand the brackets for your answers to parts **ii** and **iii**.

Practice
11C Expand and simplify

Expand and simplify these expressions.

1 a $4(x + 5) - 2x$ **b** $5(2y + 1) + 2y - 3$ **c** $4 + 3(2s + 1)$
   d $-3(t + 4) + 7t$ **e** $5(2r - 1) - 12r - 3$

2 a $6 + 2(3y + 4)$ **b** $7 - 2(m + 3)$ **c** $10 - 5(x - 1)$
   d $9g - 2(g + 3)$ **e** $p - 4(2 - p)$ **f** $5w - 3(3w + 1)$

3 a $4(x + 3) + 2(x - 2)$
   b $2(i - 1) + 3(2i + 1)$
   c $6(f - 2) + 3(2f + 5)$
   d $7(3h + 2) + 3(2h - 9)$

4 a $5(n + 3) - 3(n + 1)$
   b $7(a + 3) + 3(a - 8)$
   c $4(r + 2) - 2(r - 3)$
   d $3(2k + 1) - 2(k + 4)$
   e $4(3j - 2) - 5(2j - 3)$
   f $2(2f + 7) - 6(f + 2)$

Practice
11D Change of subject

Rewrite each formula as requested.

1 a $v = m - 10$ Make m the subject.
   b $P = Q + 5$ Express Q in terms of P.
   c $A = 3b$ Make b the subject.
   d $N = \frac{C}{4}$ Express C in terms of N.

2 **a** $f = g + h$ Express h in terms of f and g.
     b $s = vt$ Make t the subject.
     c $e = T - d$ Express T in terms of e and d.
     d $E = \frac{F}{r}$ Make F the subject.
     e $q = 3r + h$ Make h the subject.
     f $U = d - 4m$ Express d in terms of U and m.

3 **a** $M = 2n + 6$ Make n the subject.
     b $H = 5h - 20$ Express h in terms of H.
     c $w = 7 + 8k$ Make k the subject.
     d $v = 5t + u$ Express t in terms of v and u.
     e $h = 10b - c$ Make b the subject.

4 **a** $V = 6bh$ Express b in terms of V and h.
     b $n = 3g + 2b$ Make g the subject.
     c $P = abc$ Express c in terms of P, a and b.
     d $L = 5m - 5n$ Make m the subject.

5 You are given the formula $K = 6e + n$.

     a Calculate K when $e = 24$ and $n = 40$.
     b Express e in terms of K and n.
     c Calculate e when $K = 131$ and $n = 29$.

6 The time, T minutes, needed to roast a joint of lamb weighing w kg is given by the formula $T = 40w + 20$.

     a Calculate the time needed to roast a joint weighing 2.5 kg.
     b Make w the subject of the formula.
     c Calculate the weight of a joint that needs roasting for 80 minutes.

7 There are n Twinklers in each pack. Boxes contain m packs.
The total weight of a box of Twinklers is given by the formula $W = 30mn$.

     a Calculate the weight of a box containing 30 packs, given that each pack contains 4 Twinklers.
     b Express m in terms of W and n.
     c A box weighs 3750 g. Each pack contains 5 Twinklers.
How many packs are in the box?

8 The number of people, N, needed to harvest a crop of olives in t days is given by the formula $N = \frac{24}{t}$.

     a How many people are needed to harvest the olives in 3 days?
     b Rearrange the formula to make t the subject.
     c How long would 4 people take to harvest the olives?

11E Graphs from linear equations of the form $y + Ax + B = 0$

1 Rearrange these equations of straight lines to make y the subject.

    a $y - 3x + 5 = 0$ **b** $y - x - 2 = 0$

    c $y - 0.5x - 3 = 0$ **d** $y - 10x + 1 = 0$

2 **i** Rearrange the equation to make y the subject.
    ii Copy and complete the table of values.
    iii Draw each of the graphs using the axes shown.

    a $y - 4x - 4 = 0$

x	0	1	2	3	4
$y =$					

    b $y - 3x - 2 = 0$

x	0	1	2	3	4
$y =$					

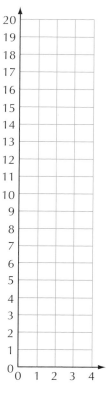

3 Copy the grid from question 2.

    a Draw the graphs of these straight lines.
        Draw all of the lines on the *same* axes.
        i $y - x - 2 = 0$ **ii** $y - 2x - 2 = 0$
        iii $y - 3x - 2 = 0$ **iv** $y - 4x - 2 = 0$
    b What is the same about each graph?
    c What is different about the graphs?

CHAPTER 12 Revision

12A Fractions, decimals and percentages

Do not use a calculator for the first four questions. Show your working.

1 **a** **i**   What fraction of this shape is pale
            orange?
      ii Convert your answer to a decimal.
      iii What percentage of the shape is pale
            orange?
   b **i**   Estimate the fraction that is dark orange.
      ii Is more than one fifth of the shape dark
          orange?

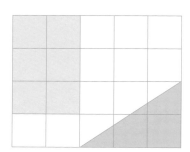

2 The three paint tins are identical. The fractions show how much paint each tin contains.

1/4 full of white paint

2/5 full of blue paint

empty mixing tin

a What fraction of the tin containing blue paint is empty?
b How much more blue paint than white paint is there?
c A full tin has a capacity of 600 ml.
How much paint is in the blue-paint tin?
d Moira pours the paint from the first two tins into the mixing tin.
What fraction of the mixing tin is filled with paint?
e Altogether, Moira has $2\frac{3}{4}$ tins of white paint and $1\frac{5}{6}$ tins of blue paint.
How many tins of paint does she have altogether?

3 Tobo used 1.7 kg of sugar to make some plum jam, and 0.8 kg of sugar to make some apricot jam. Work out the following using kilograms.

a How much sugar did he use altogether?
b He opened a new 4.1 kg bag of sugar to make the jam.
How much sugar was left over?
c Sugar costs 80p per kilogram.
What is the cost of a new bag?
d Tobo made 5.76 kg of jam altogether.
He filled 9 identical jars with the jam.
How much jam did each jar contain?

4 The diameter of the planet Mercury is 38% of the diameter of Earth. The diameter of the Earth is 12 756 km.

a Round 38% to 1 significant figure.
b Round 12 756 km to 1 significant figure.
c Use your approximations to estimate the diameter of Mercury.

5 Estimate answers to these.

a 38×63 **b** $\dfrac{31.7}{3.1 \times 1.8}$

You may use a calculator for the remaining questions.

6 There are 450 spectators at an annual cricket club match.

a 32% of the spectators were club members.
How many club members attended?
b 198 of the spectators were women.
What percentage of the spectators were women?

7 a i How much VAT at 17.5% is paid on the MP3 player?
ii What is the total cost of the MP3 player?
b What is the cost of the headphones, after the discount?

MP3

£38 plus VAT

£12.75 8% off!

8 The table shows the value of Tim's shares.

Share	Number of shares	Price of a share	Total value of shares
FirstBank	400		£3300
Pinwheel	50		£853
PowerCo	2000		£3720

a Copy and complete the table.
b Pinwheel shares increased in value by 2%.
What is the total value of Tim's Pinwheel shares?
c PowerCo shares decreased in value by 8%.
What is the total value of Tim's PowerCo shares?

Practice

12B Four rules, ratio and directed numbers

Do not use a calculator for the first five questions. Show your working.

1 **a** Put the correct sign, < or >, in between each pair of numbers.
   i −4 ... −2   **ii** 9 ... −9   **iii** −7 ... −10
  b Copy and fill in the missing numbers.
   i $260 + \boxed{} = 442$ **ii** $293 = \boxed{} - 144$

2 **a** Calculate:
   i $18 - (9 \div 3)$ **ii** $(2 \times 3^2) - 1$ **iii** $36 \div (17 - 8)$
  b Insert brackets to make each equation true.
   i $24 \div 4 + 4 = 3$ **ii** $4 + 2 \times 3 = 18$

3 Calculate these.
  a $-5 - 4$ **b** $2 - -3$ **c** $4 \times (-3)$ **d** $-21 \div -7$

4 Terri is making cheesecakes.
Each cheesecake has a pastry
shell with filling.

a Terri made a batch of pastry
weighing 490 g.
How much flour did she use?
b She used 500 g of butter to
make another batch of pastry.
How much pastry did she make altogether?
c How much of each ingredient does she need to
fill 5 cheesecakes?

Pastry recipe

Flour : Butter
= 5 : 2

Filling recipe
for one cheesecake

Soft cheese	200 g
Sugar	75 g
2 eggs	
Soured cream	125 ml

5 Calculate these.
  a 32×0.7 **b** $18 \div 0.2$ **c** 0.3×0.02

You may use a calculator for the remaining questions.

6 Which perfume is cheaper?

7 Copy and complete the table which shows details of some lorry journeys.

Journey	Distance travelled	Time taken	Average speed
Marston to Surfley	80 miles	2 hours	
Deechurch to Creek	50 km		10 km/h
Penwood to Scotbridge		15 minutes	40 mph

8

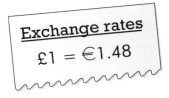

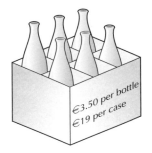

a Tamsin converted £200 to Euros to buy some wine.
How many Euros did she receive?
b She bought as many bottles of wine as possible.
How much wine did she buy?
c i How much money did she have left over?
  ii Convert your answer to British pounds.

Practice

12C Basic rules of algebra and solving equations

Do not use a calculator. Show your working.

1 a Copy and complete this sequence of calculations.

$3^2 - 1^2 =$

$4^2 - 2^2 =$

$5^2 - 3^2 =$

$6^2 - 4^2 =$

b Describe the sequence of answers to your calculations.
c Describe a rule to find the answer without squaring the numbers.
d Use your rule to find the answer to $15^2 - 13^2$.

2 A carton holds V cl of apple juice.
Write an expression for the amount of juice contained in these.

   a 3 cartons.
   b A bowl containing 3 cartons of apple juice and 50 cl of orange juice.

3 Solve these equations.

   a $5d = 30$ **b** $m + 12 = 21$ **c** $\frac{p}{3} = 7$
   d $s - 3 = 17$ **e** $3x + 4 = 22$

4

> **FOR HIRE**
>
> **£3** per day
>
> **£16** per week

   a Write down a formula for calculating the cost of hiring the cement mixer for w weeks and d days.
   b Use your formula to calculate the cost, £C, of hiring the cement mixer for:
      i 3 weeks and 2 days   **ii** 90 days
   c Martin pays £108 to hire the cement mixer for w weeks and 4 days.
      i Write down the equation.   **ii** Solve your equation to find w.

5 **a** Given that $a = 2$ and $b = 3$, evaluate these expressions.
      i $5a + b$ **ii** b^2 **iii** $3(a + b)$
   b Expand and simplify these expressions.
      i $2(x + 4)$ **ii** $5(p - 1) - 3p$ **iii** $12(t + 1) + 3(t + 2)$
      iv $5(m + 2) - 3(m - 1)$

6 The diagram shows a betting game. To play the game costs x pence.
A coin is tossed onto the board. The winnings are shown on the board.

   a Paddy flips a coin onto area A five times in a row. Write an expression to show how much he won altogether. Simplify your expression.
   b He then flips a coin onto area D once. Write an expression to show his total winnings. Simplify your expression.
   c Paddy wins 80p altogether. Write an equation involving x. Solve your equation to find the amount it costs to play the game.

Do not use a calculator. Show your working.

1 **a** Write down the coordinates of the three points.

   b **i** Copy the diagram.

   ii Add point D to the diagram so that ABCD is a parallelogram.

   iii Write down the coordinates of D.

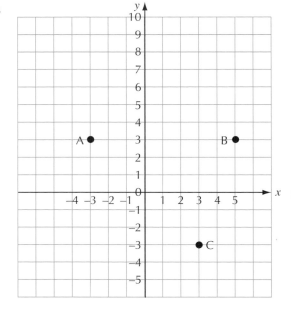

2 Match each line to an equation.

$x = -3$
$y = -3$
$y = x$
$y = 4$
$x = 4$

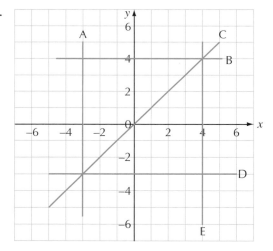

3 **a** Copy the axes in question 2.

   b Copy and complete the table for the line $y = 2x - 2$.

x	−1	0	1	2	3	4
$y = 2x - 2$	−4				4	

   c Draw the line with equation $y = 2x - 2$.

   d Where does this line intersect the y-axis?

   e Does the point (10,15) lie on the line? Explain your answer.

4 The graph shows the depth of water in an outdoor swimming pool at the end of each of the first 11 days of June.

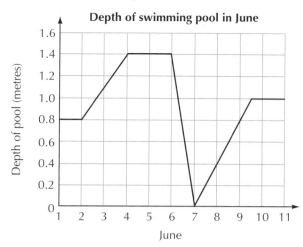

Depth of swimming pool in June

a On which day was the pool emptied?

b It rained on two consecutive days. When did it rain?

c **i** How long did it take to refill the pool?

  ii By how much did the depth increase per day?

d When did the depth of the pool change the fastest?
Give a reason for your answer.

5 The chart shows legal gun ownership and crimes involving firearms from 1979 to 1992.

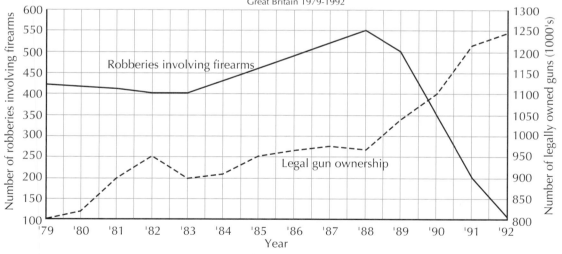

Legal gun ownership and robberies involving firearms
Source: http://members.aol.com/gunbancon/gifs/robbery.gif
Great Britain 1979-1992

a How many guns were legally owned in 1983?

b What is the difference in legal gun ownership between 1983 and 1988?

c How many robberies involving firearms were there in 1983?

d When was the fastest increase in legal gun ownership?
Explain your answer.

e *'During the period 1983 to 1988, legal gun ownership increased and so
did crimes involving firearms. This shows that legal gun ownership leads
to an increase in gun crime.'*
Do you agree? Give a reason for your answer.

You may use a calculator. Show your working.

1 Copy these grids.

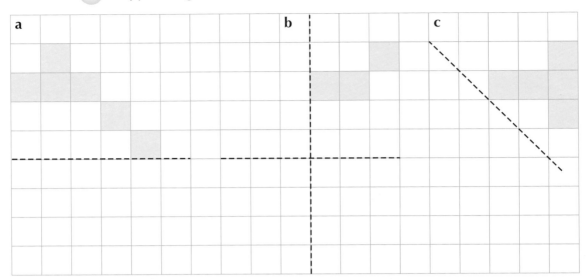

Add more black squares so that the dashed lines are lines of symmetry.

2 Copy these shapes.

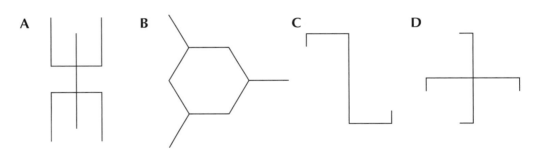

a Use dashed lines to show any lines of symmetry.
b Write down the degree of rotational symmetry below each shape.
Mark the centre of rotation using a dot.
c Copy shape C again. Add more lines to give the shape exactly two lines of symmetry.

3 a Which of the marked angles are:
  i obtuse
  ii reflex
  iii acute?
b Calculate the marked angles.

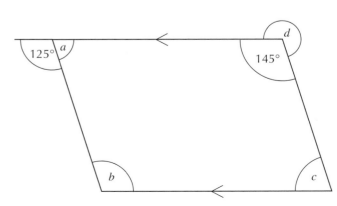

4 **a** Construct this triangle accurately.
   b Measure the side AC.
   c What type of triangle is this?

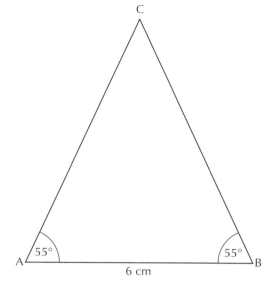

5 Do regular hexagons tessellate? Illustrate your answer with a diagram. Use triangular grid paper.

6 The diagram shows a brick and a patio made using this type of brick.

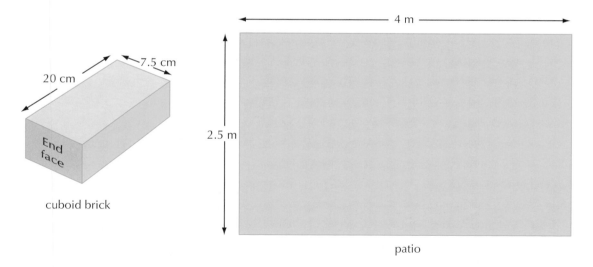

cuboid brick

patio

a Calculate the area in cm^2 of the top of the brick.
b The area of the end face of the brick is 30 cm^2.
   Calculate the height of the brick.
c Calculate the volume of the brick.
d Calculate the area of the patio.
e Estimate the number of bricks needed to cover the patio area.

7 **a** Describe the transformation that maps shape P onto shape Q.

b Copy the diagram, without shape Q.

c Reflect shape P in the *x*-axis.
Label the image R.

d Enlarge shape P using centre X and a scale factor of 3.
Label the image S.

e Rotate shape P 90° clockwise about the centre (−4, 3).
Label the image T.

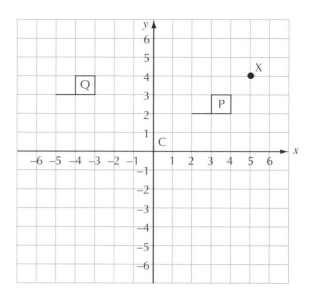

12F Handling data

You may use a calculator. Show your working.

1 These two spinners are spun together.
List the possible outcomes, e.g. (Peter, Promise).

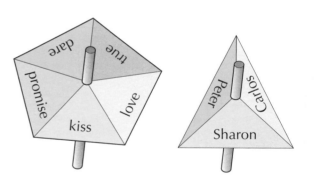

2 The table shows the badges of some girl scouts.

Badge	Adventure sports	Camera shots	Dance	Folk arts	Pet care	Total
Number of scouts	9	5	12	7	3	
Sector angle						

a Copy and complete the table.
b Draw a pie chart for the data.
Use a radius of 6 cm.
Show the angles on your diagram.

3 The table shows the time it takes to fly between cities.

	Amsterdam	Cairo	Chicago	Delhi
Cairo	4h 20m			
Chicago	8h 35m	18h 40m		
Delhi	8h 15m	7h	20h 5m	
Hong Kong	15h 15m	10h 55m	17h 5m	6h 5m

a How long does it take to fly between
  i Chicago and Amsterdam
  ii Hong Kong and Delhi
b How long is a return journey from Delhi to Chicago?
c How long is a round trip from Hong Kong to Chicago to Cairo to Hong Kong?

4 The graph shows the numbers of noise complaints in a city from 1990 to 2000.

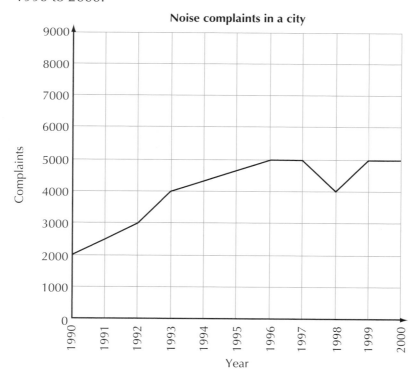

Noise complaints in a city

a How many noise complaints were there in 1991?
b In which years were there 4000 noise complaints?
c When did noise complaints fall?
d What is the difference in noise complaints between 1990 and 2000?
e When were the steepest rises in noise complaints?

5 A fruit machine has three wheels.
Each wheel has 25 symbols.
The table shows the number of symbols on the first wheel.

Symbols on wheel 1	
Apple	7
Cherry	2
Banana	4
Pear	5
Bell	1
Orange	6

a For each pull of the handle, work out the probability that the first wheel will land on:
   i a cherry   **ii** a fruit   **iii** an apple or orange

b Which of the events in question 1 are unlikely to occur?

c The probability of the second wheel landing on an orange is 0.2.
What is the probability of it not landing on an orange?

d In 20 pulls of the handle, the third wheel landed on a bell 3 times.
   i Estimate the probability of the third wheel landing on a bell.
   ii How could you obtain a better estimate?

6 StarGirl is a handheld electronic game.

a Marcus obtained these scores.

20	0	60	40
80	40	40	80
60	0	100	

Calculate these statistics:
   i mode   **ii** median
   iii mean   **iii** range.

b At the end of the game, Marcus received a bonus of 60 points.
Which of these statements are true?
   i The mode of the scores has increased.
   ii The range of the scores has increased.
   iii The mean of the scores has increased.
   iv The median has increased.

7 The diagram shows a balanced spinner and an ordinary dice.

The spinner is spun and the dice rolled together. The numbers they land on are added together.

a Copy and complete the table of possible outcomes on the next page.

b Which totals are the least likely?

c Calculate the probability of obtaining:
   i a total of 4   **ii** an even total
   iii a total of less than 6   **iv** a total that is a square number.

	Dice					
	1	**2**	**3**	**4**	**5**	**6**
Spinner **1**						
1						
2						
3						
3						

8 Hing Wai conducted an investigation into the amount of time people spend preparing and eating food. He asked ten of his teachers this question.

'How much time do you spend preparing and eating food?'

a What is wrong with this question?
b What questions would you ask?

CHAPTER 13 GCSE Preparation

Practice

13A BODMAS

Do not use a calculator. Show your working.

1 Calculate these.

    a $12 - (2 \times 4)$ **b** $3 + 4^2$ **c** $9 + (6 \div 2) + 1$
    d $6 \times 4 \div 2$ **e** $(3 \times 2) + (20 \div 2)$

2 Work out the brackets first.

    a $9 - (5 - 2)$ **b** $(16 + 8) \div 3$ **c** $(8 - 3)^2$
    d $\frac{(9 + 7)}{8}$ **e** $4(3 + 5)$

3 Calculate these.

    a $2 + (6^2 \div 4)$ **b** $3(3^2 - 1)$ **c** $10 - (9 - 6)^2$
    d $\frac{(20 - 8)}{2^2}$ **e** $4 \times \frac{15}{3}$ **f** $4^2 - (8 \div 2^2)$

4 Copy each of these equations. Insert brackets to make them true.

    a $2 + 8 \div 2 = 5$ **b** $4 + 3^2 = 49$ **c** $12 - 7 - 5 = 10$
    d $8 + 6 - 5 \div 3 = 3$ **e** $50 - 9 - 2^2 = 1$

5 Insert +, −, ÷, × and brackets to make these equations true.

a 9 ... 2 ... 3 = 15   **b** 5 ... 6 ... 1 = 35   **c** 2 ... 6 ... 4 = 2

6 Rearrange these symbols and numbers to make a true equation.

a | 3 | × | 10 | = | 2 | + | 16 |

b | 7 | − |) | = | 3 | 9 | (| − | 5 |

13B Adding and subtracting directed numbers

Do not use a calculator. Show your working.

1 The diagram shows a meter that measures volts of electricity.

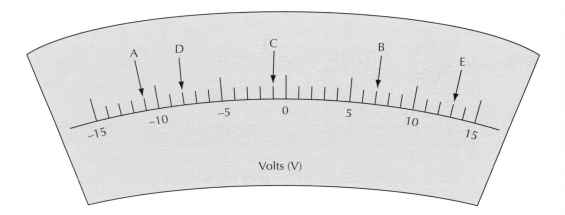

Volts (V)

a Which is the greatest of these voltages: −15, 0, −9, −4?
b Write down the voltages the arrows are pointing to.
c Calculate the difference in voltage between
   i arrows A and B
   ii C and D
   iii E and C.
d State which of the arrows point to voltages:
   i less than 7 volts
   ii greater than −4 volts
   iii less than −10 volts.
e Calculate the result of:
   i increasing −6 volts by 8 volts
   ii decreasing 7 volts by 10 volts
   iii increasing −9 volts by 3 volts
   iv decreasing −3 volts by 8 volts.

2 A dealer buys and sells antiques at auctions. The table shows the details of some antiques she bought and sold.

Antique	Purchase price, £	Selling price, £	Profit, £	Running total, £
Watch	60	50	−10	−10
Table	320	375		
Chest of drawers	565	400		
Candlestick	35		5	
Painting	145	250		
Vase	80		−3	
Victorian toy	55	80		
Set of plates	220	200		
Walking stick		6	−9	

A loss is shown as a negative profit, e.g. a profit of −£25 means a loss of £25. The last column shows the overall profit as more items are bought and sold. Copy and complete the table.

3 Calculate these.

a 2 − 5 − 9	**b** 7 − − 4	**c** (−3) + (−6)	
d − (−5) − 8	**e** 2 − +7 − 9	**f** (−4) + (−5) − (−3)	
g −2 − − 6 + 5	**h** 33 + (−54) − 17		

4 Copy and complete these equations.

a − 2 + ☐ = 6   **b** ☐ − 3 = −9

c 4 + ☐ − 2 = −3   **d** −1 = ☐ − (−3)

5 Every row, column and diagonal of a magic square adds up to the same 'magic number'. Copy and complete these magic squares.

a

−1		6
7		
−6		

b

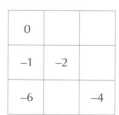

0		
−1	−2	
−6		−4

13C Multiples and factors

Do not use a calculator. Show your working.

1 Write down the first five multiples of each number.

     a 10   **b** 7   **c** 12   **d** 21

2 State the numbers in the cloud that are multiples of:

   a 6   **b** 5   **c** 8

22   30   20   72   42   45   54   18   16   24

3 **a** Find the largest multiple of 9 that is less than 80.
    b Find the largest multiple of 9 and 15 that is less than 80.

4 Here are some of the multiples of a number:

    16   32   40   64

What could the number be?
Hint: There are four possible answers.

5 The factors of a number are 1, 3, 5, 15. What is the number?

6 Write down a number less than 20 that has exactly six factors.

7 Write down all the factors of:

   a 16   **b** 26   **c** 49   **d** 54   **e** 110

8 Find the common factors of these pairs of numbers.

   a 4 and 8   **b** 9 and 12   **c** 16 and 24
   d 25 and 45   **e** 21 and 56

Practice

13D Squares, square roots, powers and primes

Do not use a calculator. Show your working.

1 Calculate these.

   a 6^2
   b the square of 20
   c 16^2
   d fourteen squared
   e $\sqrt{81}$
   f the square root of 121

Use a calculator to answer the remaining questions.

2 Calculate these correct to 1 decimal place.

   a $\sqrt{18}$ **b** $\sqrt{60}$ **c** $\sqrt{800}$

3 Calculate these.

   a 7^3 **b** 9^4 **c** 10^6 **d** 6^5 **e** 14^4

4 **a** Copy and complete the calculations.

$2^2 - 1^2 = 3$
$3^2 - 2^2 =$
$4^2 - 3^2 =$
$5^2 - 4^2 =$
$6^2 - 5^2 =$

b Describe the sequence of answers.
c Write down a rule that gives the answer without squaring any numbers.
d Test that your rule works for $7^2 - 6^2$.

5 Calculate these.

a $(-4)^2$ **b** the square of -7

6 Describe each of these numbers as odd, even, multiple, square, prime.

13   25   18   1   36   20   29   15

Example: 9 is odd, square and a multiple of 3.

Practice

13E Decimals in context - addition and subtraction

Do not use a calculator. Show your working.

1 Calculate these.

a 9.4 + 11.7	**b** 3.72 + 9.66	**c** 9.1 − 7.5
d 6.25 − 4.72	**e** 8.42 + 3.8	**f** 14 − 2.62
g 7.3 − 4.88	**h** 7.7 + 5.4 − 3.9	**i** 12.95 − 6.4 + 9.27

2 The fuel tank of a model aeroplane has a capacity of 9.25 cl. Three flights use 2.47 cl, 1.06 cl and 3.77 cl of fuel. How much fuel is left in the tank?

3 Samuel paid for a boat in three instalments: £2 319.54, £3 084.97 and £6 028.50.

a How much did he pay for the boat?
b Samuel's repayments included £482.47 interest.
How much would the boat have cost without the interest?

4 The reaction times of four people were measured.
The results are shown below.

Person	Reaction time (seconds)
Air Force pilot	0.19
Office worker	0.24
Person deprived of sleep	0.3
Person above legal alcohol limit	0.28

a How much slower was the person deprived of sleep compared to the Air Force pilot?
b Which person had the closest reaction time to the office worker: the air force pilot or the person above the legal alcohol limit?

5 The table shows the areas of the continents.

Continent	Area (millions of km^2)
Africa	30.97
Antarctica	15.5
Asia	44.49
Oceania	8.94
Europe	10.24
North America	24.45
South America	17.84

a What is the total area of Africa and Antarctica?
b How much bigger is North America than South America?
c Which two continents have the closest areas:
  i Antarctica and Oceania
  ii North America and South America?
d Calculate the total area of all the continents.

Practice

13F Decimals in context - multiplication and division

Do not use a calculator. Show your working.

1 Calculate the following.

a
```
  17.6
×    8
_____
```

b
```
 0.283
×    6
_____
```

c
```
  1.42
×   24
_____
```

d 7)90.3

e 9)0.342

f 13)1.144

2 a A chocolate biscuit weighs 12.7 g.
   How much does a packet of 6 weigh?
  b A packet of 9 shortbread biscuits weighs 0.306 kg.
   i What is the weight of a single biscuit? Work in kilograms.
   ii What is the total weight of 12 packets of biscuits?

3 A company makes a fixed charge of £18.74 per day for car hire plus 2.4p per mile. Mike hired a car for 4 days and travelled 75 miles. What was his bill?

4 Fauzia made 6.81 litres of fruit cocktail by mixing together 4 bottles of orange juice each containing 0.84 litres, and 3 bottles of apple juice. Calculate the volume of a bottle of apple juice.

5 Eight songs have a total recording time of 21.2 minutes.

    a Calculate the average length of a song, in minutes.
    b Convert your answer to seconds.

6

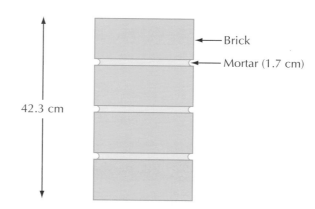

42.3 cm

Brick

Mortar (1.7 cm)

    a Calculate the total height of the layers of mortar.
    b Calculate the height of a single brick.
    c What would be the height of a wall with 24 layers of bricks?

Practice

13G Long multiplication

Do not use a calculator. Show your working.

1 Calculate these.

a	9×443	**b**	722×5	**c**	8×3283
d	7104×6	**e**	44×87	**f**	93×26
g	13×564	**h**	756×55	**i**	39×604
j	628×88	**k**	99×482	**l**	507×47
m	$22 \times 11 \times 76$	**n**	$53 \times 8 \times 87$		

2 A full matchbox contains 36 matches. A pack contains 8 matchboxes. How many matches are contained in

    a a pack?   **b** 75 matchboxes?   **c** 24 packs?

3 Shania works 28 hours a week for £7.31 per hour. Sui Main works 43 hours a week for £4.62 per hour.

    a How much does each person earn per week? Work in pence.
    b What is the difference in their weekly earnings? Work in pence.

4 Warren types 54 words per minute. How many words does he type in

    a 19 minutes?   **b** 48 minutes?
    c 2 hours?   **d** 4 hours 17 minutes?

5 The north and south sides of a stadium each have 35 rows of 126 seats. The east and west sides each have 18 rows of 199 seats. How many seats are there altogether?

6 Calculate the area of each car park.

a

96 m

234 m

b

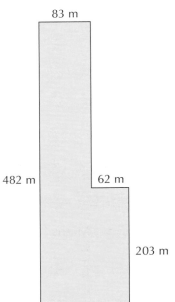

83 m

482 m

62 m

203 m

13H Long division

**Do not use a calculator.
Show your working.**

1 Calculate these. Some of the
calculations have a remainder.

a $513 \div 9$ b $\frac{857}{4}$ c $7288 \div 8$

d $\frac{9040}{6}$ e $627 \div 11$ f $429 \div 13$

g $\frac{836}{20}$ h $588 \div 21$ i $826 \div 35$

j $\frac{999}{68}$ k $693 \div 24$ l $972 \div 18$

2 **a** How many 9 cm chains can be cut from a length of 283 cm?
   b How much chain is left over?

3 12 people share a prize of £859. How much does each person receive, to
the nearest pound?

4 Which purchase is the best value? Work in pence.

SPANISH
ORANGES

Family Pack
18 Oranges for **£4.30**

SPANISH
ORANGES

Value Pack
24 Oranges for **£6.20**

5 Calculate the width of this playing field.

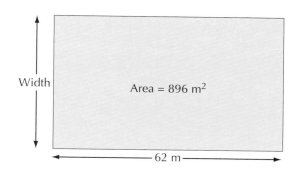

Width   Area = 896 m²

62 m

13I Problems involving long multiplication and division

Do not use a calculator. Show your working.

1 Maths Frameworking pupil books are packed into boxes of 18. Delivery vans can carry 424 boxes at a time.

    a How many books can a delivery van carry?
    b How many boxes are needed to pack 702 books?

2 These shapes all have the same area.

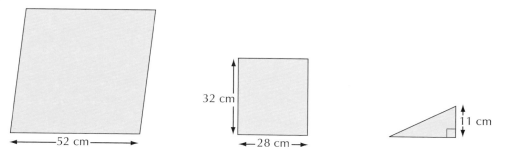

32 cm

52 cm   28 cm   11 cm

    a Calculate the area of the rectangle.
    b Calculate the height of the parallelogram.
    c Calculate the base of the triangle.

3 Hotel rooms cost £23 per person per night.

    a How much will it cost for a single person to stay for 14 nights?
    b How much will it cost for three people to stay for 9 nights?
    c Samuel's hotel bill was £552. How many nights did he stay?
    d The hotel was fully booked for three days and took £828 in rent.
        How many people stayed at the hotel each night?

4 Mariam downloaded 928 kB of data from the internet in 18 seconds.

    a How much data did she download each second, to the nearest kB?
    b How much data could she download at the same rate in
       i 45 seconds   **ii** 7 minutes?

5 Quentin used 629 cl of paint to colour 37 m² of floor. Each metre of floor is made from 16 square tiles. How much paint is needed to cover

    a one square metre of floor?   **b** a floor of area 930 m²?
    c 448 tiles?

Published by HarperCollins*Publishers* Limited
77–85 Fulham Palace Road
Hammersmith
London
W6 8JB

www.**Collins**Education.com
Online support for schools and colleges

© HarperCollins*Publishers* Ltd 2003

10 9 8 7 6 5 4 3 2 1

ISBN 0 00 713883 0

Andrew Edmondson asserts the moral right to be identified as the author of this work.

British Library Cataloguing in Publication Data
A Catalogue record for this publication is available from the British Library

Project Management and Edited by Pat Winter
Covers by Tim Byrne
Designed and illustrated by Barking Dog Art
Production by Sarah Robinson
Printed and bound by Scotprint, Haddington, East Lothian

The publishers would like to thank the many teachers and advisers whose feedback helped to shape *Maths Frameworking*.

Every effort has been made to trace copyright holders and to obtain their permission for the use of copyright material. The author and publishers will gladly receive any information enabling them to rectify any error or omission in subsequent editions.

You might also like to visit:
www.**harpercollins**.co.uk
The book lover's website